Life on an Indian Reservation

THE WAY PEOPLE LIVE

Life on an Indian Reservation

Titles in The Way People Live series include:

Cowboys in the Old West
Games of Ancient Rome
Life Aboard a Space Station
Life Aboard the Space Shuttle
Life Among the Aztecs
Life Among the Great Plains Indians
Life Among the Ibo Women of Nigeria
Life Among the Inca
Life Among the Indian Fighters
Life Among the Pirates
Life Among the Puritans
Life Among the Samurai
Life During the American Revolution
Life During the Black Death
Life During the Crusades
Life During the Dust Bowl
Life During the French Revolution
Life During the Gold Rush
Life During the Great Depression
Life During the Middle Ages
Life During the Renaissance
Life During the Roaring Twenties
Life During the Russian Revolution
Life During the Spanish Inquisition
Life in a California Mission
Life in a Japanese American Internment
    Camp
Life in a Medieval Castle
Life in a Medieval Monastery
Life in a Medieval Village
Life in America During the 1960s
Life in an Amish Community
Life in a Nazi Concentration Camp
Life in Ancient Athens
Life in Ancient China
Life in Ancient Egypt
Life in Ancient Greece
Life in Ancient Rome
Life in a Wild West Show

Life in Berlin
Life in Castro's Cuba
Life in Charles Dickens's England
Life in Communist Russia
Life in Genghis Khan's Mongolia
Life in Hong Kong
Life in Moscow
Life in the Amazon Rain Forest
Life in the American Colonies
Life in the Australian Outback
Life in the Elizabethan Theater
Life in the Hitler Youth
Life in the Negro Baseball Leagues
Life in the North During the Civil War
Life in the Stone Age
Life in the Warsaw Ghetto
Life in Tokyo
Life in War-Torn Bosnia
Life of a Medieval Knight
Life of a Nazi Soldier
Life of a Roman Gladiator
Life of a Roman Slave
Life of a Roman Soldier
Life of a Slave on a Southern Plantation
Life on Alcatraz
Life on a Medieval Pilgrimage
Life on an African Slave Ship
Life on an Everest Expedition
Life on a New World Voyage
Life on Ellis Island
Life on the American Frontier
Life on the Oregon Trail
Life on the Pony Express
Life on the Underground Railroad
Life Under the Jim Crow Laws
Life Under the Taliban

THE WAY PEOPLE LIVE

Life on an Indian Reservation

by Katherine Wagner

LUCENT BOOKS

An imprint of Thomson Gale, a part of The Thomson Corporation

APR 1 8 2005

THOMSON
★
GALE

Detroit • New York • San Francisco • San Diego • New Haven, Conn. • Waterville, Maine • London • Munich

On cover: A Navajo woman on horseback herds sheep on the Navajo Nation.

LIBRARY OF CONGRESS CATALOGING-IN-PUBLICATION DATA

Wagner, Katherine, 1957–
    Life on an Indian reservation / by Katherine Wagner.
        p. cm. — (The way people live)
Includes bibliographical references and index.
ISBN 1-59018-155-7 (hardcover : alk. paper)
1. Indian reservation—Social life and customs—Juvenile literature. 2. Indian reservation—Indians of North America—Juvenile literature. I. Title. II. Series.

Printed in the United States of America

Contents

Discovering the Humanity in Us All

Books in The Way People Live series focus on groups of people in a wide variety of circumstances, settings, and time periods. Some books focus on different cultural groups, others, on people in a particular historical time period, while others cover people involved in a specific event. Each book emphasizes the daily routines, personal and historical struggles, and achievements of people from all walks of life.

To really understand any culture, it is necessary to strip the mind of the common notions we hold about groups of people. These stereotypes are the archenemies of learning. It does not even matter whether the stereotypes are positive or negative; they are confining and tight. Removing them is a challenge that is not easily met, as anyone who has ever tried it will admit. Ideas that do not fit into the templates we create are unwelcome visitors—ones we would prefer remain quietly in a corner or forgotten room.

The cowboy of the Old West is a good example of such confining roles. The cowboy was courageous, yet soft-spoken. His time (it is always a he, in our template) was spent alternatively saving a rancher's daughter from certain death on a runaway stagecoach or shooting it out with rustlers. At times, of course, he was likely to get a little crazy in town after a trail drive, but for the most part, he was the epitome of inner strength. It is disconcerting to find out that the cowboy is human, even a bit childish. Can it really be true that cowboys would line up to help the

cook on the trail drive grind coffee, just hoping he would give them a little stick of peppermint candy that came with the coffee shipment? The idea of tough cowboys vying with one another to help "Coosie" (as they called their cooks) for a bit of candy seems silly and out of place.

So is the vision of Eskimos playing video games and watching MTV, living in prefab housing in the Arctic. It just does not fit with what "Eskimo" means. We are far more comfortable with snow igloos and whale blubber, harpoons and kayaks.

Although the cultures dealt with in Lucent's The Way People Live series are often historically and socially well known, the emphasis is on the personal aspects of life. Groups of people, while unquestionably affected by their politics and their governmental structures, are more than those institutions. How do people in a particular time and place educate their children? What do they eat? And how do they build their houses? What kinds of work do they do? What kinds of games do they enjoy? The answers to these questions bring these cultures to life. People's lives are revealed in the particulars and only by knowing the particulars can we understand these cultures' will to survive and their moments of weakness and greatness.

This is not to say that understanding politics does not help to understand a culture. There is no question that the Warsaw ghetto, for example, was a culture that was brought about by the politics and social ideas of Adolf

Hitler and the Third Reich. But the Jews who were crowded together in the ghetto cannot be understood by the Reich's politics. Their life was a day-to-day battle for existence, and the creativity and methods they used to prolong their lives is a vital story of human perseverance that would be denied by focusing only on the institutions of Hitler's Germany. Knowing that children as young as five or six outwitted Nazi guards on a daily basis, that Jewish policemen helped the Germans control the ghetto, that children attended secret schools in the ghetto and even earned diplomas—these are the things that reveal the fabric of life, that can inspire, intrigue, and amaze.

Books in The Way People Live series allow both the casual reader and the student to see humans as victims, heroes, and onlookers. And although humans act in ways that can fill us with feelings of sorrow and revulsion, it is important to remember that "hero," "predator," and "victim" are dangerous terms. Heaping undue pity or praise on people reduces them to objects, and strips them of their humanity.

Seeing the Jews of Warsaw only as victims is to deny their humanity. Seeing them only as they appear in surviving photos, staring at the camera with infinite sadness, is limiting, both to them and to those who want to understand them. To an object of pity, the only appropriate response becomes "Those poor creatures!" and that reduces both the quality of their struggle and the depth of their despair. No one is served by such two-dimensional views of people and their cultures.

With this in mind, The Way People Live series strives to flesh out the traditional, two-dimensional views of people in various cultures and historical circumstances. Using a wide variety of primary quotations—the words not only of the politicians and government leaders, but of the real people whose lives are being examined—each book in the series attempts to show an honest and complete picture of a culture removed from our own by time or space.

By examining cultures in this way, the reader will notice not only the glaring differences from his or her own culture, but also will be struck by the similarities. For indeed, people share common needs—warmth, good company, stability, and affirmation from others. Ultimately, seeing how people really live, or have lived, can only enrich our understanding of ourselves.

A Beautiful but Dangerous Isolation

The Duck Valley Indian Reservation, a 290,000-acre reservation that straddles the Nevada-Idaho border, is home to the Shoshone-Paiute people. On the Nevada side of the reservation, the tiny town of Owyhee offers residents few conveniences. It is a small town that attracts hardly any visitors from Nevada or Idaho much less people from outside the area. When *Sho-Ban News* reporter Wyatt Buchanan stopped in Owyhee in the summer of 2002, he wrote: "This is the middle of nowhere and 100 miles from any Interstate freeway or railroad track. The closest grocery store is 13 miles away. A bank and tribally owned fuel pump just recently came to town. Buying fresh meat means a two-hour drive to Mountain Home, Idaho."[1]

"The middle of nowhere" is a phrase commonly used to describe reservations, whether the reservation is tucked inside the swampy Florida Everglades or deep in the heart of the Grand Canyon or high atop a southwestern mesa. Reservations are generally sparsely populated. While most have several thousand residents, about one-fourth have fewer than fifty residents. Only one reservation, the Navajo Nation, has a population greater than one hundred thousand.

The isolation shapes the Native American way of life. Reservations are places where shepherds can be found tending their flocks. They are also places where men still follow the seasons as fishermen, trappers, and hunting guides and women make pottery in a traditional way. But reservations are also places where residents often live without basic services such as telephones because it is too expensive to run telephone lines to remote areas. About half of all reservation residents do not have telephones. The Yurok Tribe, on the Yurok Reservation in Northern California, lives in a river gorge that cuts them off from the outside world. It is so isolated that cell phones do not work there and in cases of emergency, the tribal school must use an unreliable radiophone.

For many Native Americans, however, living in an out-of-the-way location is exactly what they like best about reservation life, for as a former tribal chairman on the Duck Valley Reservation said of his home, "You can go out during the day or at night and not hear anything but the birds. I love it. It's unique, isolated."[2]

Whether they like it or not, isolation is something residents learn to live with. In many ways it sustains them, bringing family and friends closer together. Family life has always been an important part of Native American culture, and reservations have not changed that. Families spend lots of time together in daily activities such as eating meals or driving into town. This closeness extends into the community where events such as powwows and rodeos allow individuals to connect with their tribal family.

"Lonesome for the Stars"

Children who grow up on reservations feel connected not just to their extended family

A long stretch of road winds across the Navajo Nation, the largest and most populated reservation in the United States.

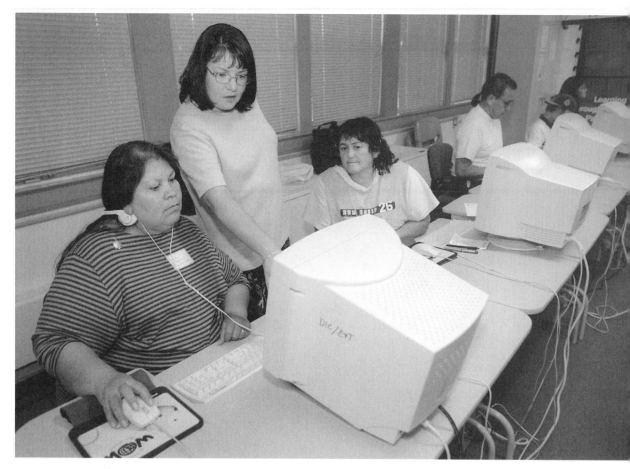

An instructor at the Denver Indian Center demonstrates how to use e-mail. Access to the Internet can ease the sense of isolation residents experience on some reservations.

but to nature. Residents are more likely to see a buffalo grazing in the prairie grass or a sunset over the Pacific Ocean than they are to see a shopping mall or electrical power line. This relationship with the natural world has a strong appeal for young Native Americans. After living in Indianapolis, Indiana, for a year a woman in her early twenties returned to her home on the Fort Belknap Reservation in Montana because city life made her, in her words, "lonesome for the stars."[3]

The pace of everyday life on a reservation is much slower than it is for people who live in urban areas. A young Navajo mother, whose home on the reservation is thirty miles away from the nearest grocery store, recalls what life was like when she lived for a time in Albuquerque, New Mexico: "I remember how it seemed everyone was so rushed. People would complain about going to the store. I drive 30 miles to the store. It's no big deal."[4]

But the remoteness of reservations is not without problems, for, as one writer put it, reservations have a "beautiful but dangerous isolation."[5] Residents must drive long distances on narrow, unpaved winding roads just to buy a loaf of bread or to get a prescription filled. Isolation also causes economic hardships. Businesses are reluctant to build plants or offices on reservations. As a result, it can be difficult to find a job, and the jobs that are available are often low paying or temporary.

A Link to the World

But life is slowly changing on reservations as new technologies allow residents to interact with the outside world. For example, communications satellite links now make it possible for reservations in the most isolated areas to offer their residents Internet service. On the remote coast of northwest Washington, the forty-seven-square-mile Makah Reservation is a two-hour drive away from the nearest city, Port Angeles. During winter, when the fishing industry slows, about half the residents of the reservation are out of work. Now, the Makah Indians are part of an intertribal program that is bringing the Internet to reservations in the Pacific Northwest. The project will create jobs, some in providing technical support for the users of the Internet service, and others that consist of tribal members selling handmade items such as woven baskets and wooden carvings through online businesses.

Yet, for all the possibilities that technology offers in the way of a better life, challenges remain. On many reservations nearly half the population is under eighteen years old. The increase in the number of children has put a strain on the services that tribal governments can provide to their communities. Funding for schools, day care facilities, and recreational programs have been stretched to the limit in reservation communities that are already among the poorest communities in the country.

In *Indian Country Today*, Delphine Red Shirt, who lives on the Pine Ridge Reservation in South Dakota, describes the common elements of reservation culture: "For me, any time I drive onto a reservation in America . . . that same feeling comes across, that feeling of entering someone's homeland, a place where a nation, a culture has existed uninterrupted for thousands of years; that feeling of shared poverty and isolation."[6]

A Host of Sovereign Governments

Reservations within the United States serve as homelands for more than 550 tribes. The lands owned by these tribes are considered sovereign nations. This means that tribes can make laws and provide services to meet the needs of their people. A writer in *Indian Country Today* notes that sovereignty is a concept with which Native Americans have long been familiar. "When the first settlers landed on North America they 'discovered' a continent that was already home to a host of sovereign governments. These tribal nations, in existence for thousands of years, were self-governing and self-sufficient."[7]

Sovereignty was something the writers of the U.S. Constitution believed was an inherent right of all tribes. As sovereign nations, tribes have a government-to-government relationship with the U.S. government. Tribal governments, therefore, can make treaties and pacts with both federal and state governments. In resolving intergovernmental issues, tribal leaders

A sign at the entrance to the Golden Hill Paugeesukq Reservation in Connecticut identifies the tribe as a sovereign nation.

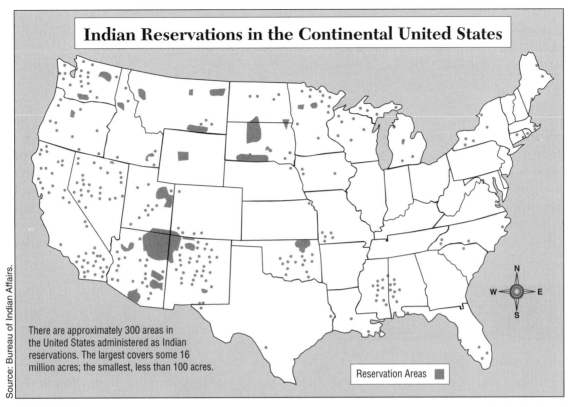

Indian Reservations in the Continental United States

Source: Bureau of Indian Affairs.

There are approximately 300 areas in the United States administered as Indian reservations. The largest covers some 16 million acres; the smallest, less than 100 acres.

Reservation Areas

meet with members of Congress, members of the president's cabinet, governors, and even the president of the United States.

Tribal sovereignty is not absolute, however. Although tribes govern themselves, they do so under the watchful eye of the federal government. Reservation land is generally held in trust for the tribes by the federal government. While tribes control the land, the government has the ultimate responsibility for ensuring that the land is protected and maintained. This responsibility is part of numerous treaties that past tribal leaders negotiated with the U.S. government.

The BIA

About 57 million acres is held in trust for tribes and individual tribal members and can only be sold with the approval of the federal government. The secretary of the interior serves as the trustee for the lands. The secretary, in turn, delegates many of the trustee's responsibilities to the Bureau of Indian Affairs (BIA). This agency of the federal government then serves as the official protector of tribal lands.

The tribal lands the government oversees reach into all corners of the country. There are more than three hundred Indian reservations in the United States. Reservations vary in size from a few acres to thousands of square miles. Most are small, however, covering an area less than fifty square miles. In some cases, the reservation is tribally owned land with few buildings and no residents, such as the Capitan Grande Reservation in eastern San Diego County. Only about 10 percent of all reservations are larger than one thousand square miles but some reservations are larger than some states. There are a dozen reservations larger than the state of Rhode Island, for instance, and nine reservations larger than the state of Delaware.

Not all reservations are part of the federal reservation system, however. There are a number of tribes that are recognized by state governments but not by the U.S. government. In such cases, the state government controls reservation lands and provides funding and protection for tribes. Some of the oldest reservations in the country are state recognized, including the 150-acre Mattaponi Reservation. (While the reservation was cre-

ated by an act of the Virginia General Assembly in 1658, the tribe was not recognized by the state until 1983.)

Tribal Powers

Although the federal government has ultimate control over tribal lands, the tribes have a number of powers. According to the Minnesota Indian Affairs Council, the powers of Indian tribes include the

power to establish a form of government;

power to determine membership;

power to police;

power to administer justice;

power to charter business organizations.[8]

Each tribe can extend its power and authority only to its own members living on the tribe's reservation. The tribe has no authority over other residents, such as people who move there from other reservations to marry into the tribe or because of a job transfer. There also are many non-Indians living on reservations. In the Midwest and Northwest, white residents on reservations account for anywhere from 3 or 4 percent of the population to as much as 90 percent. The presence of these non-Indians on reservations is the result of federal government policies. For example, in the late 1800s and early 1900s, the federal government divided reservation land into individual homesteads. After allocating homesteads to tribal members, the government allowed white settlers to buy the remaining parcels of land.

Nontribal members living on a reservation do not participate in the tribal govern-

Iroquois Confederacy

Although the U.S. Constitution serves as the basis for most tribal governments today, in the past that influence went both ways. America's founders, such as Benjamin Franklin, observed the political system of the Iroquois Confederacy, an alliance of five tribal nations in present-day New York State, and adapted some of what they learned in structuring the federal government. The confederacy consisted of the Cayuga, Mohawk, Oneida, Onondaga, and Seneca. The five tribes had a common council that included elected delegates who represented both their tribe and a clan within their tribe. The council met in long, bark-covered communal houses known as longhouses. There was no single leader of the alliance and all decisions had to be unanimous. Iroquois law remains unchanged today and still guides the Grand Council of the Iroquois people.

ment and have no say in tribal laws. However, they cannot be arrested by tribal police, nor can they be put on trial in a tribal court. In some cases, however, tribes allow non-Indians living on the reservation to attend schools on the reservation and use tribal facilities, such as community wellness centers.

Constitutions

Nearly all tribes have a form of government similar to the U.S. federal system. That is, most tribal governments have three branches: executive, legislative, and judicial. Most tribal governments are based on a constitution modeled on one that was provided to them by the BIA. Scholars say, however, that this one-size-fits-all approach has caused problems for some tribes because the model did not take into account the unique characteristics of individual tribes or historical methods of leadership. In recent years, therefore, many tribes have rewritten or reorganized their constitution to better fit their way of life. As a noted economist explains, "One type of government does not appeal to or produce positive results for all tribes."[9]

Some Native Americans believe that constitutions took the power away from the people and put it into the hands of a few tribal members. On some reservations, groups have called for changes in their tribe's constitution and have resorted to public protests to achieve their goals. One of these protests took place on the Pine Ridge Reservation in South Dakota early in the twenty-first century. A group of one hundred people, calling itself the Grass Roots Oglala Lakota Oyate, accused the tribal council of a number of misdeeds, including the mishandling of millions of dollars. The Grass Roots group seized the tribe's financial records and asked for an audit of the

records by the federal government. Despite their occupation of the tribal government's building in Red Cloud, South Dakota, for a year and a half, in January 2004 a *Native Voice* reporter included this observation in a follow-up article:

> The same problems remain firmly in place some 28 months later. There are still gaps in the systems that govern how money is accounted for and spent. Nepotism still rules the job selection process, with many positions going to family members and political supporters, many with questionable qualifications. The tribe's form of government remains unchanged.[10]

Furthermore, some Native American groups have yet to accept the constitution adopted by fellow tribes people. For example, several older villages on the Hopi Reservation in Arizona have never accepted a constitution. As Wayne Taylor, a member of the Hopi tribal council, told a reporter in 1998, "We had an election to form a constitution back in 1934. We've had a kind of rocky history with the tribal government. Not all the communities, not all the Hopis, wanted to have this government. So we have some villages that don't quite accept this government, even today."[11]

Old Oraibi

In the Hopi's case, objections to the tribal constitution are rooted in religion. A resident of Old Oraibi, one of the villages that rejected the tribal constitution, explains: "This village was created for a purpose; it has longstanding cultural roots, and we made a promise to Ma'saw [the guardian of this place] about how we would live here. . . . Ma'saw allowed us to live

The Hopi people believe their elders, like this man, have great wisdom, and they hold them in very high esteem.

here, and he is the ultimate leader here. We lied to him if we now choose another way of life. If that's the case, he may end this life for us here."[12]

Instead of being governed by the tribal authorities, the village of Old Oraibi is run by *kikmongvi*, or clan leaders. A clan is a group of people who can trace their history to a common ancestor. In Old Oraibi, the people do not elect a leader. Instead, the clan leader designates a successor. The elders say that a constitution is "not the Hopi way" and that they see no reason to abandon their traditional village leadership. As an Old Oraibi el-

der asks, "Why draft a constitution when we still have a village leader? With a constitution, the traditional leader has no authority."[13]

Hereditary Leaders

For many Native American tribes, however, the constitutional model contains elements that are, if not identical, at least reminiscent of traditional forms of leadership. Most Native Americans lived in villages, which often had alliances with other nearby villages. The villages and the alliances were governed by councils. The village councils had representatives from each family while the larger alliance councils had representatives from each of the villages.

Chiefs presided over the councils, although they generally did not have the power to impose decisions on them. Chiefs also negotiated with outside groups. How the chiefs were chosen varied. Some inherited their positions; others were chosen by the people because of some admirable deed. Chiefs, then, had limited power. Moreover, often the chief's power was limited to specific functions, such as war making.

Success of Indian Reservations

The article "Talk to Focus on Success of Indian Reservations," appearing on the Rice News Service, reports that a study by Harvard University shows that tribes can thrive economically if they are allowed to govern themselves and be accountable for their decisions.

Joseph Kalt, a Harvard University professor who has been studying social and economic development on reservations as part of the Harvard Project on American Indian Economic Development, says, "The central result of our research is that a tribe can have natural resources and financial capital, but if there is not a stable institution of tribal government and a rule of law, then its resources will be wasted." Kalt goes on, "The successful tribes are set about much like countries in Eastern Europe—they are rebuilding court systems, tax systems, and regulatory systems."

Indian tribes are working to restructure government systems, such as courts of law. Pictured is the Pima-Maricopa Indian Community court building in Arizona.

On the Lower Sioux Reservation in Minnesota, two tribal elders give the following account of the tribal decision making process in a traditional Dakota community, which the elders say included input from the entire tribe:

Families were the foundation of all relationships. Extended family formed the foundation of and made rules for the band. A council of 10 to 20 people from different bands, situated itself in a special lodge in the middle of a camp made up of the various bands. The council discussed everything. One of its primary responsibilities was to care for the elderly, poor, and handicapped within the bands. No one member of the council had more power than another. Each band had a crier who told everyone about decisions made by the council.[14]

Enforcement of decisions made by a governing council or a chief was often the responsibility of the warrior society, whose members generally had proved themselves through some act of bravery, passing an initiation ritual, or both. Members of the warrior societies were often expected to possess admirable qualities beyond bravery. For example, according to an Arapaho elder on the Wind River Reservation, the warriors were often the poorest people in the tribe because they were always giving to the tribe.

Traditional Leaders Help Out

While traditional chiefs and warrior society leaders no longer run tribal affairs directly, they still play an important role in keeping tribal governments running smoothly. For instance, on the Northern Cheyenne Reservation in Montana, the council of forty-four hereditary chiefs, along with warrior society leaders, helps to settle disputes and resolve problems on the reservation. When, in February 2003, the eleven-member tribal legislature accused the tribe's president of disregarding the constitution and mismanaging tribal funds, it was the hereditary chiefs who helped forge a solution. The hereditary leaders met separately with the legislature and the president. The hereditary leaders were able to convince both parties to let the matter be resolved in court. "As chiefs and society headmen, our job is to provide a peaceful resolution,"[15] said Leonard Elkshoulder, a member of the council of forty-four traditional chiefs.

The legislature and president were grateful for the intervention of the hereditary leaders. "I respect the societies and the chiefs. They came here in a humble way to help the executive branch and legislative branch come to some common ground,"[16] said the tribal president, Geri Small.

Tribal Councils

The number of tribal council members depends on the size of the tribe. For instance, the tribal council on the Pine Ridge Reservation has eighteen members while the smaller Caddo Reservation in Oklahoma has five members. Council terms generally last for two years or four years.

The exact structure of tribal government is also variable. As an example, the Viejas Band on the Viejas Reservation in San Diego has two levels of government: the general council and the tribal council. The general council includes all of the band's 157 adult voting members and elects the tribal chairman. The general council also votes on all decisions affecting the use of reservation land. The tribal council, which consists of just six

Lawmakers sit in the Navajo Nation Council Chamber in Window Rock, Arizona. The large Navajo Nation has a complex system of tribal governance.

members, governs day-to-day tribal activities and makes laws.

With over one hundred thousand residents, the Navajo Nation faces a much more complex situation than the Viejas Band faces when it comes to governance. The Navajo Nation has a tribal council of eighty-eight members who are elected from districts, or chapters, as they are known. Each chapter consists of about two thousand people and elects one delegate to the tribal council.

The chapter is the connection between individual citizens and the tribal council. Within each small community on the Navajo Nation is a "chapter house," which serves a function similar to that of a town hall. Several times a month, community members meet at the chapter house, where they discuss issues pertaining to the community and action they would like the tribal council to take.

Communal Living

Tribal members generally want their governments to make decisions based on traditional values. For example, historically Native Americans lived communally and individuals shared their resources with other tribal members. Today, tribes still consider property communal and believe that tribal money should be shared communally. Some tribes own and operate businesses, such as casinos, which generate large profits. In general, the profits are split between the tribal government and individual tribal members. The individuals are free to spend their share as they wish. The tribal government uses the money to improve the quality of life on the reservation as a whole.

Profits of tribally owned businesses, such as casinos, are usually distributed equally to all tribal members. This process does not always run smoothly, however. For example, in Colorado, on the Southern Ute Reservation, the Southern Ute Tribe has a number of businesses, including a natural gas company, that generate monthly payments for tribal members. Some members, however, claim that payments are not equal and that tribal council members are getting more than their fair share of the profits. In addition, some people say that business decisions are made without the input of tribal members. At times, council meetings have turned into shouting matches as tribal members accuse tribal officials of unfairly distributing money that belongs to the tribe.

On many reservations the tribal council oversees the work of an administrative staff, that handles the day-to-day responsibilities of running the reservation. The tribal government is broken down into departments, that manage a wide variety of programs and services, including social services, health services, law enforcement, business development, and education. At times the list of departments can be extensive. As an example, the Hoopa Valley Reservation in California has twenty-five hundred residents and a tribal government that has sixty departments.

Historically the BIA managed most of the services and programs on reservations, but since the 1970s tribal governments have assumed responsibilities that had previously been the province of the BIA. The exact programs that are handled by the BIA and those that are managed by the tribe vary from reservation to reservation, although poorer and smaller tribes usually rely more on the BIA for administrative aid.

Tribal Membership

One of the most important functions tribal governments now perform is that of deciding who is part of a particular tribe and therefore entitled to live on tribal lands and receive tribal benefits. In the past, the BIA determined the criteria for tribal membership, but now that task is left up to the individual tribes. Tribal councils oversee membership enrollment and base their decision on a number of factors, such as shared customs, traditions, languages, and kinship.

Tribes have different ways of deciding who qualifies for membership. Many require a certain percentage of tribal blood. For example, the Kiowa Tribe of Oklahoma requires individuals to possess 25 percent Kiowa blood to qualify for membership. The Cheyenne-Arapaho Tribe of Oklahoma is a bit more restrictive, requiring not just that an individual have 25 percent tribal blood, but that at least one parent be an enrolled member of the tribe. In contrast, any descendent of a tribal member qualifies for membership in the Cherokee nation in Oklahoma. Not all tribes require individuals to have tribal blood. For example, someone can become a member of the White Mountain Apache Tribe if the individual is over twenty-five years old, speaks Apache, and lives on the reservation or runs cattle on tribal land.

Tribal membership is not, however, irrevocable. Tribal councils can, and sometimes do, change the rules for membership, resulting in individuals losing their status as tribal members. When this happens, individuals lose their claims to tribal land and benefits.

Just such a situation arose in the late 1990s, when fourteen members of the Paiute Tribe in Nevada learned that they no longer qualified for tribal membership even though many of them were longtime community members who had served on prior tribal councils. The individuals who lost their membership said that the changes to the member-

Tribal Businesses

On many reservations the tribal council oversees new business development on the reservation and serves as a board of directors for tribally owned businesses. In some cases, the tribal president's job resembles that of a company president or CEO. On the San Manuel Reservation in California, Tribal Chairman Deron Marquez works up to ten hours a day, six days a week, managing the tribe's various business ventures, including a casino, water-bottling plant, hotel-restaurant complex, and community center.

ship requirement were part of a long history of power struggles among families in the fifty-four-member tribe. The members who were disqualified had few options to gain reinstatement since tribal councils have the sole power to determine tribal membership.

A member of the Paiute Tribe recalls how she felt when she received the news that her membership had been terminated: "When I got the letter stating I was disenrolled, I couldn't believe it. I've been a Paiute all my life. It was the worst day of my life. It was like they took part of my heart and ripped it out."[17]

Law Enforcement

Although some aspects of tribal leadership mirror traditional practices, other aspects are reflective of non-Indian practices. For instance, tribal governments no longer rely on warrior societies to protect residents, relying instead on tribal police departments. Still, these law enforcement agencies tend to reflect the values of their communities and work hard to be a part of those communities.

Such community policing programs are based on the idea that close bonds between police officers and residents help officers both prevent and solve crime. The tribal police departments on the Flathead Reservation in Montana and the Umatilla Reservation in Oregon have both adopted the community approach. Police officers patrol a designated area of the reservation on a daily basis. In most cases, the officers live in the community they patrol.

As part of the program, the officers are encouraged to develop relationships with community members. To do this, the officers attend community events, such as wakes and funerals, district meetings, senior citizens'

meetings, crime prevention meetings, and school lunches. In some cases, the contact between the officers and residents is more personal. For example, on the Caddo Reservation in Oklahoma, police officers are required to check in on elderly residents from time to time to see how they are doing.

Tribal Court

Just as many tribal police departments adopt methods that will benefit the community, the tribal courts emphasize arriving at decisions that benefit all parties involved. The courts handle a variety of cases, including those that deal with drug possession, child custody issues, and land disputes. However, serious vi-

Tribal police maintain close ties with the community. Here, officers are sworn in on the Fort McDowell Yavapai Reservation in Arizona.

Two attorneys for the Navajo Nation organize their notes before a special session of the Navajo Nation Supreme Court. The proceedings in this case were held at Harvard University in Massachusetts.

olent crimes such as murder are usually handled in federal courts.

Tribal courts often reflect the small, intimate communities they serve. The atmosphere usually is relaxed and informal. There may be minimal security, perhaps just one unarmed bailiff. Tribal court judges pride themselves on keeping the atmosphere in their courtrooms friendly. Rather than wearing robes, judges often wear casual clothes. Rather than sitting on raised podiums, they sit at tables that are at eye level with the people in the courtroom. Even if the courts have an informal atmosphere, however, there are reminders that the court is an arm of a tribal government. The courtroom features the tribe's flag, and the tribal emblem seal replaces the U.S. seal behind the judge's podium.

At the same time, tribal courts also reflect traditional values. The way tribal courts deal with juvenile crime and delinquency often reaches back to traditions of involving the entire community to help a member in trouble. For example, in the Strong Heart Court on the Spokane Reservation in Washington, teams of ten people work together to decide the best course of action in dealing with juvenile crime. Team members include prosecutors, drug counselors, probation officers, defense attorneys, tribal elders, and other tribal members. Each team member gets to vote. The presiding judge must abide by the wishes of the majority, even if the judge does not agree with the decision.

As sovereign nations, Native American tribes can determine their own fate. To be successful, tribes have found that they need to establish strong governing systems that create business and education opportunities on the reservations that will lead to self-sufficiency for tribal members.

Education

M ost Native Americans recognize that the key to self-sufficiency is having a skilled and educated populace. Historically, however, accomplishing this goal has challenged Native Americans, who have the highest school dropout rate of any ethnic group in the United States. In some communities as many as 60 percent of Native American children leave school before graduating from high school. Many tribes are working to reverse these numbers. To accomplish this, tribal governments are taking control over

Students on the Spokane Indian Reservation learn to use computers. Tribal schools generally follow the same curriculum as other schools.

the schools on their reservations and, in the process, creating educational systems that match the community's needs.

The School System

Like other services on Indian reservations, schools and educational activities are overseen by the federal government. The Bureau of Indian Affairs, therefore, is the federal agency responsible for educating Native American children who live on reservations. The BIA sets the academic standards for the schools and provides money for teachers' salaries and for building construction and maintenance. In the past, the federal government also directly operated all the schools in the reservation system. Since the 1970s, however, tribal governments have assumed most of the responsibility for day-to-day management of the BIA schools on reservations.

The BIA funds schools across the country, on sixty-three reservations in twenty-three states. The majority of the schools are located in the southwestern states of Arizona and New Mexico, with the Navajo Reservation having the greatest number. Reservations in North and South Dakota have the second largest concentration of schools. Most of the schools are for students in kindergarten through eighth grade; for high school, most reservation youngsters attend a public high school off the reservation.

The BIA school system serves a diverse population of sixty thousand students from 250 tribes. The local tribal school districts are free to set the requirements for enrollment and some choose to enroll only students who are Native American. For example, the Muckleshoot Tribal School on the Muckleshoot Reservation in Washington requires students to be members of a federally recognized tribe.

In Mississippi, students who attend Choctaw Central High School on the Pearl River Reservation must be at least one-fourth Native American. Some tribal schools, however, accept non-Indian children who live on the reservation or in a nearby community. At the Joseph K. Lumsden Bahweting School on the Sault Sainte Marie Reservation in Michigan's Upper Peninsula, about 30 percent of the 270 elementary school children are non-Indian.

The Classroom

Bahweting, like other reservation schools, has smaller class sizes than most public schools. At Bahweting, there are typically eighteen children in a class. Some reservation schools have even smaller classes; at Indian Island School on the Penobscot Reservation in Maine, most classes have fewer than ten children. The small class size allows teachers to spend time with each child, going over lessons or talking about problems that the student might be having at home.

Children in tribal schools study the same subjects as schoolchildren around the country. Elementary and middle school students take classes in language arts, social studies, and math. Students attending those high schools that are located on reservations study subjects such as English, accounting, geography, algebra, biology, and history.

In addition to the standard courses, schools also offer cultural programs in which children learn about their ancestral literature, history, and language. These types of programs are generally only a small part of the school day. Even so, Native American educators say the programs are important because, as John Bear Mitchell, native studies teacher at Indian Island School, says, "teaching students about their culture instills pride and leads to greater academic success."[18]

The Indian Island School and the Beatrice Rafferty School on the Pleasant Point Passamaquoddy Reservation in Maine both have cultural programs. As part of the programs, tribal words appear on hallway bulletin boards and on classroom walls. At Beatrice Rafferty, the day begins with a student reciting the Passamaquoddy word of the day over the school's public address system. In addition, at Indian Island, the library has student-designed tapestries that depict the totem animals of the different clans within the tribe.

The Teachers

At Indian Island, the cultural program teacher is a tribal member. Even so, only six out of seventeen teachers at the school are Native American. Most teachers at reservation schools are non-Indians. As an education official who is a descendent of the Chickasaw and Choctaw tribes recalls, "As a child, I never had an American Indian teacher."[19]

Non-Indian teachers in reservation schools find themselves hampered if, as is often the case, they lack an understanding of their students' culture and the role that culture plays in how children learn. In some cases, tribes offer programs to raise cultural awareness among teachers. The Page school district, for example, sponsors a one-day orientation for new teachers, where speakers discuss different aspects of Navajo life and stories about the reservation. Speakers explain that in their society, children learn by observing their elders and then repeating what they see.

A non-Indian teacher who participated in the orientation offered this observation of how her Navajo students behaved in the classroom: "I would tell you that most of my students are listeners and watchers. They

Cross-Cultural Ties

One letter started a cross-cultural exchange that brought together young people from Bavaria, Germany, and students from the Santee Reservation, Nebraska, home of the Sioux Tribe.

In 1999 German dental technician Peter Pfaffinger, who leads a group of scouts, sent letters to fifty North American tribes looking for a partnership with the young people in his organization. The only tribe that responded to the request was the Santee.

After a lengthy correspondence, twenty students from Santee Tribal School traveled to southern Germany, where they hiked the Alps and toured a castle. They also performed their native singing and dancing for the Bavarian state minister. The German government helped pay some of the travel expenses for the Santee students.

After that, twenty-four German teens came to the United States to visit the Santee Reservation. During their stay they slept in a tepee and attended a rodeo. For Pfaffinger, the person responsible for the cross-cultural exchange program, the trip to Nebraska fulfilled a childhood dream. In an article entitled "A Child's Dream Becomes a Rare Exchange Between Two Cultures" in *Indian Country Today*, Pfaffinger says that Germans have a special interest in American Indians. "Maybe it is a dream of ours to ride on the back of a horse, have a tipi, and be free," he says.

A Native American teacher hugs a student at a school on the Spokane Reservation. Most teachers on reservations are not Native Americans.

learn by watching, mostly . . . they rarely ask questions as they have been taught to watch how to weave, watch how to make pottery, watch how to make silver jewelry, watch how to tend sheep, and watch how to participate in family chores."[20]

If finding teachers who understand Native American culture is a challenge for school administrators on the reservations, low pay and remote working conditions make it difficult to attract and retain teachers at all. Math and science positions are the hardest positions to fill, since the supply of qualified applicants tends to be small. For example, the Standing Rock Reservation in North Dakota advertised for several months for a science teacher without one person applying for the job.

Tribes employ a number of strategies to cope with recruiting qualified teachers. One school on the Rosebud Reservation has been able to hire teachers from India. The Wellpinit School District on the Spokane Reservation succeeded in attracting Native American teachers to its staff by offering them subsidized housing on the reservation.

Sometimes, volunteerism helps fill the need for teachers. This is particularly the case in schools that various churches operate on reservations. Typically, volunteers serve for a

School buildings are often decorated to reflect Native American culture. The school mural on Wyoming's Wind River Reservation features Indian motifs.

limited time—perhaps a year or two—and receive no more than a stipend to cover living expenses. Such volunteers, however, rarely can afford to stay long enough to truly become a part of the community in which they serve.

The tribal schools also make use of volunteers who, by assisting teachers and other school staff, help chronically cash-strapped schools stretch their budgets. Many of the volunteers are part of the AmeriCorps program, a federal program that sends college-age students to help out in communities around the country. In the spring of 2004, for example, nine AmeriCorps volunteers spent six weeks working at the Tohaali Community School on the Navajo Nation Reservation. The school provided housing and lunch for the volunteers, who tutored in the classrooms and cleaned up the school's nearly century-old apple orchard.

The School Buildings

Finding teachers is only one problem plaguing reservation schools. On many reservations, the schools themselves are in dire need of repairs. On the Crow Creek Reservation in South Dakota, for example, many of the school's aging buildings have been condemned. The situation is so bad that the high school gymnasium can no longer be used for school or community activities. Instead, the tribe must pay rent to nearby schools for the use of their gymnasiums.

The school funding, however, is uneven, resulting in the more fortunate reservations being able to build schools that are up-to-date. When Jonathan Eig, a reporter for the *Wall Street Journal*, visited the Pine Ridge Reservation, he noted that the high school was a modern brick building trimmed with a colorful design that resembled a beaded headband. Inside, the school was "equipped with most of the modern conveniences: computers, color copiers, Internet connections and paper-towel dispensers that activate automatically when hands pass before them."[21]

Some schools are able to offer students access to state-of-the-art technology. The Spokane Reservation tribal school provides a personal computer for each of its five hundred students and e-mail access for students in grades four through twelve. Students at the Bahweting School can conduct their science experiments on Palm Pilots, which are issued by the schools.

While the newest technology can sometimes be found inside the schools, building designs often look back in time to incorporate traditional Native American culture. When a new elementary school was being built on the Navajo Nation Reservation, community residents offered input on the design to ensure that the building would include elements of the Navajo culture. As a result, the building's green and orange colors blend into those of the surrounding countryside and the school's entrance is shaped like a hogan, a dirt-covered cone-shaped log structure that the Navajo traditionally used for their homes.

Not every tribe can afford up-to-date school buildings, much less state-of-the-art computer hardware. On reservations where money is tight, classes are often held wherever space that can be used as a classroom is available. On the Kootenai Reservation in Idaho, for example, twenty-three children attend elementary school in a blue double-wide mobile home.

Long Bus Rides

The students at the Kootenai trailer school, however, are fortunate in that they live within

Science Fair Winners

Looking for a solution to the housing shortage on their reservation, four students from the Crow Reservation won a twenty-five-thousand-dollar grant in a national science competition. Lucretia Birdinground, Omney Sees the Ground, Kimberly Deputee, and Brenett Stewart all worked together on a project to build homes using bales of straw.

The middle school students, who all attend Pretty Eagle Catholic School, constructed a demonstration model of a straw-bale home. The girls then subjected the house to a number of tests, including trying to set it on fire with a blowtorch. The students concluded that straw-bale buildings are economical, energy efficient, and fireproof.

As part of the winning grant, the four girls helped build a straw-bale recreation center on the reservation.

An online Web site is giving a voice to Native Americans attending tribal colleges. RezNet (www.reznetnews.org) pays students to report about events happening on their reservations and at their colleges.

The students write about news, sports, culture, and student life. There is also a movie review section called Frybread Flicks. RezNet articles have included a story about two boxers who stepped into the ring at a tribal college to raise money for a poetry club and an interview with a Navajo man running for mayor of a town next to the Navajo Nation.

walking distance to their school. The reality for most students is long daily bus rides to and from school. On some reservations children spend up to six hours a day commuting between home and school.

More than three-quarters of the fifty-six hundred children who attend Pine Ridge tribal schools travel to and from school by bus. In his article about the high school on Pine Ridge Reservation, reporter Jonathan Eig writes that students have at least an hourlong bus ride every morning: "In winter, students board buses before dawn. By the time they make the 30- or 40-mile trip to school, the sun is up and the snow-covered buttes that dot the landscape surrounding the school have turned from gray to white."[22]

When they can, tribes build new schools with an eye to limiting the amount of time students spend traveling to and from school. The Pala Tribe, located in rural San Diego County, decided to build a new school to help reduce the commuting times for children on the reservation. Building the school eliminated bus rides that had been as long as forty-five minutes for some students.

Sometimes a tribe simply cannot afford to offer daily bus service to children who live in isolated corners of the reservation. In such cases, children live in dormitories close to their school. In all, more than eleven thousand elementary and high school students live in dormitories while attending schools on the reservation or in off-reservation districts.

Children who attend such boarding schools spend the school week away from their homes. For example, in Montana, the St. Labre Indian School is a Catholic school system that serves seven hundred elementary students on the Northern Cheyenne and Crow Reservations. The school's policy requires students who live more than forty minutes from the school to live in the dormitories during the week. The children arrive at the dorm by bus on Sunday night and return to their families on weekends and school breaks.

In some cases the federal government will step in when students do not have a school that is a reasonable distance from their homes, forcing a public school district off the reservation to provide a school for reservation children. In the mid-1990s, for example, the Department of Justice sued a school district in Utah because the children from the Navajo and Paiute tribes living in the remote community of Navajo Mountain did not have a school near their homes. To attend school, children had to travel more than ninety miles each way, live with a relative, or live in a dormitory at the school. The court ruled that the school district had to build a high school for the students, just as it had done for other non-Indian children who lived in remote regions of the district.

Skipping Classes

While ensuring that students have a school nearby is an important goal of most tribes, an even bigger challenge is making sure that students come to school. Truancy is a common problem throughout the Native American community. At any one time as many as 40 percent of reservation children who should be in school are not. Students skip classes for a number of reasons. In many cases it is because of a situation at home, such as having to help take care of younger brothers and sisters.

Students who do not attend classes often find themselves falling behind on their schoolwork and simply give up and drop out of school. Native Americans have a high dropout rate, with roughly 50 percent of high school students failing to graduate. On some reservations, the dropout rate is even higher. Of the two hundred freshmen who enter Pine Ridge High School each year, for example, only about eighty eventually graduate.

It is unclear why there is such a high dropout rate, but some educators are working to find out. In Maine, the principals of Indian Island School and the Beatrice Rafferty School on the Passamaquoddy Reservation have developed a system to track students once they leave elementary school and enter nearby public high schools. The study will pinpoint which students excel at the high school level and which ones fail. The principals hope the information will help them understand what they can do for their students to make sure they complete their high school education.

The president of the board of education on the Passamaquoddy Reservation believes that students from small reservation schools, such as Indian Island and Beatrice Rafferty, are not always ready for the leap to high school. "A lot of them aren't prepared," she says. "A lot of them are scared. A lot of them have to work twice as hard, and they don't have the support at home stressing how important education is."[23]

Going Away to College

Although many Native American teenagers drop out, some students work hard in school because they see education as a ticket out of a life of poverty on the reservation. In the Pacific Northwest, Glenda DeLaMater from the Chehalis Reservation in Washington attended Bacone College in Oklahoma when she was only sixteen years old. After graduating with honors from high school, DeLaMater earned a scholarship to Bacone. She says that a fourth-grade teacher inspired her to work hard in school: "She told me every day that I was one of the kids that was going to make it in college."[24]

Being so far away from her family and friends was difficult for DeLaMater. Even though the school's enrollment is 50 percent Native American, she says she is not like the other students. "I'm a northwest Indian, and these (at Bacone College) are southwest Indians. There's a big difference: our cultural beliefs are different, our dances are different, our songs and outfits are different."[25]

Despite the hardship of living two thousand miles away from home, DeLaMater feels that her life is better than it would be on the reservation. After she graduates from college, she will look for a job off the reservation. "There is no opportunity on the reservation," she says. "It seems everyone on the reservation is stuck there. I wanted to leave and make something of myself to show everybody it can be done."[26]

Tribal Colleges

Most Native American teens who want to attend college must leave the close-knit communities where they grew up. However, tribal colleges offer students an alternative to traditional off-reservation institutions. Because the colleges are located on reservations, they provide students with the chance to pursue an education without having to leave familiar surroundings. As a slogan for the Denver-based American Indian College Fund (AICF) says: "Lots of kids go to college so they can leave home. (Indians) go to college so they can stay home."[27]

Having a college on the reservation does not, however, guarantee that students have an easy time. In fact, many of the students are single parents, and they endure great hardships just to attend. One reporter praised the students at Oglala Lakota College on the Pine Ridge Reservation for their persistence. "They hitchhike to get to class. Lean on family members to baby-sit their kids. Study in cold rooms with outdated books. And, in doing so, these American Indian students are becoming what they never thought they would be: college graduates."[28]

By all accounts, tribal colleges succeed at keeping students in school. According to the

There are thirty-five tribal colleges, and the number is growing. Pictured is the college on Montana's Rocky Boy Reservation.

American Indian Higher Education Consortium in Washington, D.C., there is a 90 percent dropout rate for Native American students who go from high school to an off-reservation college or university. But students who attend tribal colleges have a 90 percent completion rate.

Students do better at tribal colleges because they are around people who understand and respect their culture, explains an administrator at the Bay Mills Community College on the Bay Mills Reservation in Michigan's Upper Peninsula. As an example, tribal colleges accommodate students who want to take time off from school to participate in rituals and ceremonies. Deborah Pine, a graduate from Bay Mills Community College, says: "The administrators . . . understand that if I had to leave for a week to go, say, attend a funeral—a traditional Indian funeral with the feast and ceremonies—I may need to leave right away and be gone for awhile. I don't have to explain."[29]

The goal of students who attend tribal colleges is to gain marketable job skills. The schools, therefore, offer vocational training intended to help graduates find jobs both on and off the reservation. Students can take courses in nursing, heavy equipment operation and repair, environmental studies, and social work. Graduates often find work on the reservation as dental assistants, construction workers, native language teachers, and forestry managers.

In addition to job training, the tribal colleges help students reconnect to their tribal culture. At the Saginaw Chippewa Tribal College in Michigan, students can take classes in drumming and alabaster sculpture, traditional Ojibwa arts. An instructor at the school says that his students "are interested in regaining their culture. They're drawn to learn about Ojibwa arts and traditions by what we call 'blood memory'—by the spirit that is inside them and has never been lost."[30]

Students at Bay Mills Community College learn about Native American history. Students are required to take classes in the history and organization of Michigan Indian tribes. A history teacher at the school explains how the courses at Bay Mills differ from those at mainstream colleges:

A lot of students in my Western Civilization course are surprised to discover that there was a thriving city of 30,000—Cahokia—located in Illinois, back during the 13th and 14th centuries. While Europe was going through the plagues of the medieval period, this group of Mississippians [Indians] had built a sophisticated culture, complete with temples and a priest-based religion.[31]

Classes at Bay Mills are typical of those at other tribal colleges in that they combine classroom study with activities designed to enhance an understanding of tribal culture. The school offers a language instructor program to help prepare students to teach Nishnaabemwin, the Ojibwa language. Students enrolled in the program spend the morning studying Nishnaabemwin grammar. After class they go outside to hike on nearby trails. As they walk, the students converse in Nishnaabemwin while they learn the native names for the plants and animals they see along the way. The students also pick sweetgrass, which they later weave into baskets in the traditional way.

Tribal colleges do more than just educate students; they also help boost economic and business development on the reservation. Several schools have started construction companies that are intended to keep money on the reservation instead of having it leave to

Tribal governments offer classes that teach useful skills to local residents. Here, Zuni Pueblo men work in a furniture-building apprentice program.

off-reservation businesses. At the Sitting Bull College on the Standing Rock Reservation in South Dakota, students and graduates of the school's building trade program have worked on a number of construction projects including new student housing on the campus. At the Salish Kootenai College on the Flathead Reservation in Montana, students enrolled in the college's trade program helped to build most of the school's buildings, including ten classroom buildings, a bookstore, a water quality lab, an administrative building, and a clubhouse at the college's golf course.

While tribal colleges provide training to local residents, tribal governments also offer programs to give residents the education and skills they need to fill jobs on the reservation. On the Tulalip Reservation in Washington, community leaders have created a construction training program. The tribe is building a new outlet mall on the reservation and hopes to add more tribal members to the construction crew. Over the course of the sixteen-week training program, students learn how to take measurements correctly and how to read blueprints.

In Connecticut the Mashantucket Pequot Tribe has a program to ensure that tribal members will qualify for jobs on the reservation. The tribe offers a mentoring program, which pays the college tuition for young people and then offers them entry-level positions with the tribal government or at the casino and resort the tribe operates. The program allows participants to select jobs from a variety of fields including accounting, health care, hospitality, and business administration. Job placements range from working as an assistant in the casino's human resources department to working as a masseuse or masseur in the tribal health spa. In addition, members can work at the Mashantucket Pequot Research Center and Museum as archeologists, anthropologists, and historians.

In some cases tribes offer apprenticeship programs, which combine training and work experience. On the Stillaguamish Reservation in Washington, young tribal members serve as apprentices in a plant nursery on the tribe's fifty-six-acre farm. The apprentices, who range in age from sixteen to twenty-five, learn about propagating plants, tending gardens, potting, planting, and fertilizing. The tribe also offers a training program for Native American youths from the reservation and surrounding areas, finding participants internships at retail stores and manufacturing plants.

Casinos such as this one at the Mille Lacs Reservation in central Minnesota provide employment to many tribal members.

In Arizona, on the Gila River Indian Reservation, the Tohono O'odham Tribe has started to develop several programs that give young people hands-on experience in operating a business. The tribe maintains a garden at the reservation school where students grow specialty crops, such as herbs and squash blossoms, to sell to restaurants on the reservation. High school students learn about the restaurant business in a training program that allows them to earn credit and get paid for part-time jobs at the school's café. The tribe hopes that when the students graduate from high school they will hold management positions at the tribal casino or nearby restaurants.

Graduates of tribal schools and colleges serve their communities as writers, scientists, teachers, small-business owners, and government employees. Beyond providing vocational training, the purpose of the reservations' schools and colleges is to reconnect young people with their roots and prepare them to become the business leaders of the future.

Making a Living

Although tribes are developing programs to expand the number of businesses on the reservation, most residents find it difficult to find a job near their homes. Few, if any, large companies are based on tribal lands. As a result, on some reservations the unemployment rate is as high as 70 or 80 percent. Moreover, reservation jobs are often low paying or seasonal and offer limited opportunities for promotion.

Government Jobs

Because there are so few private companies operating on the reservations, the majority of residents work for public agencies. One of the largest is the tribal government, which employs administrative assistants, clerks, secretaries, and bookkeepers. Not all tribal employees work in offices, however. Some tribes employ groundskeepers to mow grass, trim trees and shrubs, plant flowers, and pick up trash. Still other tribes hire individuals to service and repair equipment.

Many people are employed by the schools. Those with the right qualifications work as teachers or principals; others work as teachers' aides, cooks, and janitors. Most reservation communities also offer Head Start classes, a federally sponsored preschool program for children from low-income families. Head Start

Tribal office employee Randy'L He-dow Teton prepares tribal documents. Tribal governments provide many jobs for Native American residents.

provides jobs in some of the most remote regions. For instance, in the tiny community of Red Shirt on the Pine Ridge Reservation in South Dakota, the program has five employees, including teachers, a part-time cook, and a bus driver.

Although substantial numbers of reservation residents work directly for the tribe, the largest employer on reservations is the federal government, especially the Bureau of Indian Affairs. Because the BIA operates a wide variety of programs, it offers jobs in fields as varied as archaeology, maintenance work, soil conservation, and fire management.

Firefighters

On many reservations tribal members hold seasonal jobs as firefighters for the BIA forestry program. For Native Americans, fighting forest fires is more than just a way to make money. "Indians have a lot of pride and tradition in fighting fires,"[32] says Randy Pretty on Top from the Crow Reservation in Montana. In many cases, firefighting is a tradition passed down in families. For example, on the Crow Reservation, firefighter Twilla Pretty Weasel's father was a firefighter and today Pretty Weasel works on the same crew

A Crow man takes a break from his firefighting duties. For many tribes, firefighting is a tradition passed down through generations.

Members of the Hoopa Valley Tribe in California study logging activities on their reservation. Many reservation residents work with federal agencies in land conservation.

as her two grown sons, who are also firefighters.

Working as firefighters on the reservation can dovetail nicely with Native American traditions. For example, Calvin Becenti, manager of the BIA's Navajo forestry program, notes that there are traditional Navajo ceremonies that involve participants sleeping outside on the ground in all types of weather and wearing the same clothes for days at a time, circumstances similar to what firefighters encounter when they are battling a wildfire.

Becenti also contends that the native firefighters, when faced with dangerous conditions, rely on a sixth sense, a feeling that the Navajos have when they "close their eyes and see with their spirit."[33] This sixth sense has earned Native American firefighting crews the respect of government officials at the national level. Jim Stires, the head of the fire management branch of the BIA in Washington, D.C., says, "We have some real high-

level, sophisticated computer modeling to understand fire behavior, but if a veteran Indian firefighter told me what a fire was going to do, I'd believe him over the computers."[34]

Land and Wildlife Jobs

In addition to the BIA, there are a number of other federal agencies that offer jobs in land and wildlife conservation and protection. Among these are the Bureau of Land Management (BLM), the U.S. Fish and Wildlife Service (USFWS), and the National Park Service (NPS). These agencies oversee federally managed forests, wildlife refuges, and parklands. Some of these areas are located on reservations. For example, parts of the National Bison Range and Glacier National Park lie within the boundary of the Flathead Reservation in Montana.

These federal agencies generally hire seasonal workers, but residents who have specialized skills or college degrees can sometimes find year-round employment. Typically, the BLM employs environmental engineers, foresters, and technicians. The USFWS hires biologists and technicians to conduct wildlife habitat restoration projects and seasonal wildlife surveys. The NPS hires park rangers, law enforcement officers, guides, firefighters, and administrators.

Reservation residents who have at least some post–high school training in a scientific field can sometimes find work with other federal agencies, such as the Environmental Protection Agency (EPA), which hires people to monitor the air and water quality on reservations. Residents of the nineteen pueblos, or reservations, in northern New Mexico often commute to nearby Los Alamos National Laboratory, where they find work as technicians. Los Alamos is the federal research facility where the first atomic and hydrogen bombs were developed in the 1940s and 1950s, and where today research is being done in high-speed computing, lasers, and environmental technologies.

Health Care Jobs

Another federal agency that provides jobs is the Indian Health Services (IHS). This agency oversees hospitals and health clinics on reservations. Qualified Native Americans find work as doctors, nurses, physical therapists, pharmacists, and medical records technicians. In addition, nearly 90 percent of the administrative staff are Native American.

Because many reservations typically are short of medical personnel, employees often work long hours. Monica Mayer, a member of the Lakota Tribe who grew up on the Pine Ridge Reservation in South Dakota, returned to her home after receiving her medical degree. Reporter Dorreen Yellow Bird describes what Mayer's workday was like when she first came back to the reservation and held jobs at the hospital in Stanley and the health clinic in New Town at the same time: "Her clinic hours were 8 A.M. to 5 P.M., with an hour to race 35 miles to the Stanley hospital, where she worked the night or until 8 A.M. Then, she returned to New Town to begin her clinic for the day there."[35]

In general, anyone with professional training who works on an Indian reservation can expect long hours and little chance for vacations. Ethel Johnson, a veterinarian on the Blackfeet Reservation in Montana, is on call twenty-four hours a day, seven days a week. Johnson is one of two veterinarians on the 1.6-million-acre reservation. She runs a veterinary clinic, providing health care to animals on farms and ranches within sixty miles of her home. She has one full-time assistant and two part-time students helping in the clinic.

Working long hours or doubling up on duties is not done just by medical professionals. At some schools where money is tight, teachers take on tasks outside the classroom. At the Kootenai Tribal School on the Kootenai Reservation in Idaho, the native language teacher makes soup and sandwiches for the students' lunches and helps out with the janitorial work. At the All Tribes American Indian Charter School on the Rincon Indian Reservation near San Diego, the school's principal also serves as a bus driver, teacher, and cafeteria cook.

Part-time Job, Double Duty

Although they work long hours to earn their pay, full-time employees find that pay is often lower compared to similar jobs elsewhere.

Those who cannot find a full-time job face even more difficult circumstances, since they often must work two jobs to make ends meet. On the Navajo Nation Reservation, Isabelle Walker held two part-time jobs, one as a district leader for the Navajo government and another as a representative for the Indian Health Services. Walker's jobs required her to travel to different locations on the sprawling reservation. In all, she drove about twelve hundred miles a week. That much time on the road took Walker away from her family, forcing her to choose between spending time with her family and meeting her work obligations.

In some cases tribal members are unable to find work on the reservation at all and must drive long distances for jobs at mining sites, manufacturing plants, and sawmills. Sometimes residents take temporary jobs that are too far to commute to on a daily basis. Those who work in construction are particularly apt to face this situation, living away from home for the duration of the job. On the Pine Ridge

A Native American health-care worker visits the home of a patient on the Hoopa Valley Indian Reservation in northern California.

Many Native American tribes are developing businesses that provide earth-friendly alternative energy to the reservation and beyond. Tribes across the country are tapping into the power of the natural resources around them to create jobs and income.

In Washington State members of the Tulalip Tribe are experimenting with using manure from dairy cows as an energy source, while in New York the Seneca Nation is investigating water- and wind-generated power.

In the Southwest the Navajo Nation is developing solar energy operations to bring power to ten thousand homes on the reservation.

In the Great Plains a 170-foot wind turbine is generating electricity to 325 homes on the Rosebud Reservation in South Dakota. The Blackfeet Tribe has a wind farm with fifteen turbines on its Montana reservation. The wind farm employs five workers and provides power to six thousand homes in Oregon and Montana.

Reservation, for instance, tribal members often live and work in Rapid City, about 120 miles away, for part of the year.

Long Commutes

In most cases, whether they work on or off the reservation, people spend several hours a day commuting to and from their jobs. In Idaho, Nez Perce tribal chairman Samuel Penney drives sixty-six miles to work every day. As he makes his daily morning journey along the Clearwater River to the tribal headquarters, he travels from one end of the 770,000-acre reservation to the other.

Because most reservations are so sparsely populated, commuters do not have to deal with rush hour traffic or frequent stop signs or stop lights. However, reservation roads are often poorly maintained with the result that even a short drive can take a long time. Many roads are also hazardous, especially when it rains or snows.

In fact, one of the greatest concerns of reservation residents who work is getting to

their jobs. Only a few reservations have public transportation systems. Even if individuals live within walking distance of their jobs, few reservations have accommodations for pedestrians, such as sidewalks. A woman on the Navajo Reservation recalls what it felt like when she did not own a car and had to walk to and from work: "I was walking home and it rained. And there was this one car and it zoomed by me and it splashed mud on me, I said 'Oh no!' And I was praying, 'Lord, I need a car. I need a car. I don't want to be like this. It's cold and I'm having all these problems.'"[36]

For some residents the solution to the transportation problem is to work at home. In this respect, those who earn a living making handicrafts have an advantage. In his home workshop at Taos Pueblo in New Mexico, artist Dukepoo makes silver rings, bracelets, belts, and pendants. He and his wife travel to craft fairs, powwows, and various other events around the country to sell his creations. Although Dukepoo and his wife travel a good deal, they are able to maintain a home in Taos Pueblo, a community of 150 that otherwise offers little in the way of employment opportunities.

Yellow Sky

Those who work in native crafts often are participating in long-held family traditions. For example, Yellow Sky, a potter on the Santa Ysabel Reservation in California, learned how to make red clay pots from his grandmother. He uses traditional techniques, such as firing the pots in a fire pit at his home. Inside the pit he puts chunks of evergreen bark on top of small pieces of wood and then covers that with chunks of dried cow manure. The fire makes the black designs on the red pot. One of the most striking pots he made had a lone black star on it. "The fire makes them black," Yellow Sky says. "A lot of pictures come out in the design. The fire does that."[37]

Handicrafts are labor-intensive. The pots Yellow Sky makes sell for anywhere from three hundred to nine hundred dollars a piece, but they require about four days to complete. Other Indian craftspeople earn even more money from their creations, although they may invest long hours in a single item.

A Navajo woman weaves a blanket. The Navajo have long been known for their woven blankets and rugs.

Rug weaver Sarah Natani, who lives on the Navajo Nation Reservation, carries on a tribal tradition. The Navajos are known for their woven rugs and blankets. Natani, who is in her sixties, weaves two to three hours a day in the kitchen of her hogan. One of her four-foot-by-five-foot rugs can take months to make but sells for as much as six thousand dollars.

Doll Maker

While many Native artists work at traditional crafts to make a living, others artists use more modern techniques to depict some aspect of traditional Native American life. Jamie Okuma, a twenty-four-year-old award-winning artist, uses her artistic skills to create soft sculpture dolls. Okuma shares a trailer home with her parents on the La Jolla Reservation, which covers nine thousand acres in Southern California and is home to about four hundred members of the La Jolla Band of Luiseño Indians.

To make her dolls, Okuma spends much of her time researching historical Native American clothing. One of her dolls, which was sold to a collector, depicts a nineteenth-century Sioux woman in her traditional style of clothes complete with an intricately beaded purse.

Chet Barfield, a reporter for the *San Diego Union-Tribune*, wrote this description of Okuma and her workspace:

> Petite and soft-spoken, she has red-dyed streaks in her hair and a silver stud in her tongue. She likes to go surfing with friends at Torrey Pines beach.
> Her studio is a 10-by-20-foot shed of unvarnished wood. Inside are her workbench, her tools, her soldering torch.

Boxes of fabric are stacked near a surfboard, a microwave oven and a case of Red Bull energy drink.[38]

Traditional Farmer

Like the artists who work from their homes, Native American ranchers and farmers support themselves and their families without having to commute to work. Ranching and farming are common in the Southwest. For many, farming is not their only job. They may have a small plot of land that they tend, but they work elsewhere and supplement their income with whatever they can grow on their farm.

Historically, reservations were created on land that white settlers had little use for. This means that the soil is generally of poor quality. Furthermore, Native American farmers, especially those in the Southwest, often find that water is in short supply. Many small farmers belong to cooperatives, which share water resources from tribal irrigation projects.

Despite the hardships, Wilbur Charleston, a farmer on the Navajo Reservation, plants crops such as corn, squash, and melons, using traditional Navajo methods. After digging six-inch holes in the ground with a shovel, he puts sheep manure on the bottom of the hole and then puts in the seeds. "Our grandfathers and grandmothers knew that the best way to plant around this area of the country is to dig holes and plant the seeds deep," he says. Charleston's wife and two children help him with the planting. He says the work brings them closer together. "When you plant a seed and then watch it grow as a family, there's something special that happens between you and your wife and your children."[39]

Every August, Native American artists come to Santa Fe, New Mexico, to sell their hand-made items at the Santa Fe Indian Market, the largest such event in the country. The market attracts one hundred thousand visitors and twelve thousand artists from one hundred tribes. The artists must submit proof of their tribal membership before they are allowed to participate in the show.

Goods for sale at the market include silver jewelry with inlaid turquoise, pottery, baskets, woven rugs, blankets, and sculptures. One of the most popular items is the kachina doll, a carved and painted figurine that represents one of a variety of spirits in the religion of the Pueblo people in the Southwest.

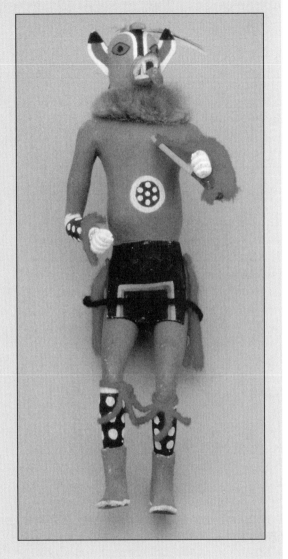

Kachina dolls are popular items for many collectors of Native American art.

Gila River Farm

While Wilbur Charleston has a small, single-family farm, the Tohono O'odham Tribe in Arizona operates a large-scale farming operation on the Gila River Indian Reserva-tion, which provides food for residents and businesses on the reservation. The sixteen-thousand-acre farm produces a variety of crops traditionally grown in the area, including cotton, alfalfa, small grains, melons, citrus fruits, and olives. In the winter months, the farm provides pasture where cattle and sheep can graze. In all, the farming operation employs approximately 140 full-time workers, including a farm manager and an assistant farm manager, and 250 part-time employees.

The farm, along with a nearby fish farm, supplies food to the Kai Restaurant, part of the Sheraton Wild Horse Pass Resort and Spa located on the reservation. The tribe also operates a produce market that sells items such as fruits, hay, and olive oil to locals and tourists.

Navajo Shepherds

The Gila River Farm is helping to ensure the survival of traditional crops, but in most communities traditional agriculture is in danger of fading away. On the Navajo Reservation, for instance, the Navajos are losing their pastoral way of life, according to Navajo Nation president Joe Shirley Jr. Shirley says that only a few families living on the Navajo Reservation still have herds of at least one hundred or two hundred sheep. "To have that, that is independence," Shirley said. "You can stand on your own feet."[40]

Sheep herding as a way of earning a living is becoming increasingly rare in the Navajo Nation, in part because young people no longer want to live that kind of life. Writer Betty Reid moved away from the Navajo Nation, where she grew up, to take a job as a journalist in Phoenix, Arizona. Back on the reservation, Reid's mother and aunt, both in their seventies, tend a flock of sheep in the traditional Navajo way.

Reid drives to the reservation every weekend to help her mother and aunt, who divide their time between Tuba City, a town on the reservation, and a sheep herding station thirty miles away. Reid's mother and aunt now look after a flock that includes only seventeen sheep and one goat. At one point in the past, the two women had as many as four hundred sheep. The sheep provided many of life's necessities. In the spring the sheep were sheared for their wool, which the two women used to weave rugs. The sheep also served as food and as barter for necessities the women could not produce. Reid's mother sees her way of life fading away. Since ownership of sheep traditionally is passed down to the younger generations, Reid's mother worries about the future of her flock. Speaking in the Navajo language, Reid's mother asks: "I imagine my life and that of the sheep will end soon. Who will take care of the sheep?"[41]

The Return of the Buffalo

Whereas some tribes keep alive the tradition of sheep herding, others are making a living raising a powerful symbol of Native American culture, the buffalo. At one time there were millions of buffalo in North America. Many tribes relied on these animals for food and as a source of hides, which they used for clothing and shelter. European settlers slaughtered the buffalo until only a few thousand remained. Buffalo are being reintroduced on reservations across the country as both a potential income source and as a way to bring back one of the most important symbols of Native American life. The total buffalo population in the United States and Canada stands at 350,000.

Today fifty-two tribes in eighteen states have buffalo herds. The largest herd, consisting of twenty-four hundred animals, is on the Cheyenne River Reservation in South Dakota. One of the smallest is a herd of twenty-six in the Picuris Pueblo in New Mexico. Like other tribes, the Picuris have a bison manager, who is responsible for making sure that the herd is safe and healthy.

The buffalo, for centuries a powerful Native American symbol, is being reintroduced on reservations as a source of income and tribal pride.

The Lakota people on the northern plains have always felt an especially close kinship with the buffalo. Sheldon Fischer, the wildlife specialist on the Lower Brule Sioux Reservation in Montana, expresses how many American Indians feel when they see buffalo: "I can't explain it but to say I feel at peace," he says. "They are magnificent animals. We can learn a lot from them."[42]

The tribes involved in raising buffalo are hoping that the meat can be sold and that the herds will be a tourist attraction. About fifty tribes, including the Lower Brule Sioux Tribe, have formed the Intertribal Bison Cooperative in Rapid City, South Dakota. The cooperative distributes buffalo and buffalo meat to tribal communities, schools, and the elderly who might otherwise not receive adequate nutrition.

Of additional interest is the possibility that eating buffalo meat may help Native Americans prevent and control diabetes. Native Americans have the highest rate of the disease in the world. Dieticians believe this

The Grand Pequot Casino is a resort on Pequot land in Mashantucket, Connecticut. Indian-owned casinos provide steady income to many reservations.

has been caused by a shift from traditional low-fat foods, such as buffalo meat, to processed foods, which are high in fat and sugar. Tribal communities have responded by developing programs aimed at promoting traditional foods, including buffalo.

Casinos

Some Native Americans say that the buffalo has been replaced as the mainstay of tribal economies. The replacement is the casino, which, just as buffalo did for many tribes before Europeans arrived, provides Native Americans with a means of survival. Not only do casinos offer job opportunities to some residents of the reservations, profits from the gaming and resort operations help support various tribal activities. In all, there are about two hundred Indian-owned casinos in the country.

In fact, the value of the casinos is not so much the jobs they provide for tribal members but rather the profits they generate that can be reinvested. Although casinos provide jobs in security, human resources, and dealing, many of these jobs are held by non-Indians who live on the reservation or in nearby communities. For example, in one tribal casino in California, only two out of fifteen hundred employees were tribal members.

Profits can be reinvested in other tourism-related businesses, such as the casinos themselves, hotels, or golf courses, or they can be used to develop factories. In Washington State, the Tulalip Tribe used its casino money to develop a commercial center where retail stores such as Home Depot and Wal-Mart provide jobs for reservation residents.

Other Businesses

While some tribes have profitable casino operations, this is not the case on all reservations. Generally only casinos near large urban centers do well. Tribes on remote, isolated reservations cannot rely on getting enough visitors to support a casino. They must develop businesses that take advantage of the natural resources found on their reservation.

In the Pacific Northwest, where seafood is readily available, the Jamestown S'Klallam Tribe owns and operates the Jamestown Seafood Company. The reservation is located along the coast of Washington. Tribal members dive seventy feet into the ocean waters of

This large clam is known as a geoduck. Members of the S'Klallam Tribe on the Washington coast gather these clams to sell to restaurants.

the Puget Sound to collect a popular type of clam known as geoduck. The company also sells Dungeness crabs and Manila clams. The seafood is shipped to customers in California, New York, and around the world.

Some of the new businesses focus on traditional uses of resources found on the reservation. For example, in Arizona, Bill Quiroga is running a business selling medicinal herbs from his trailer home on the Pascua Yaqui Reservation. For generations, Native Americans have used herbs to prevent and treat illnesses. Quiroga received money from his tribe to research different methods to grow the plants, which he hopes to sell to both Indian and non-Indian customers.

The Nez Perce tribe is also returning to a tribal tradition by running a horse-breeding program on its Idaho reservation. The program has eighty horses and two full-time employees. Native American teenagers help out in the summer. The young people haul hay, clean out stalls, and practice their riding skills as they learn to take care of the horses in a traditional way.

Tourism

Some tribal businesses are taking advantage of the fascination that Native American culture holds for some non-Indians by offering tourists the opportunity to vacation on a reservation. Visitors come from as far away as Europe to experience the natural beauty on reservations. Just two examples of such vacations are a rafting trip down the Colorado River with a Hualapai guide or a fishing trip on the Pamunkey Reservation in Virginia.

In South Dakota, Alex White Plume owns and operates Lakota Pony Rides, a company that allows visitors to experience the solitude and quiet of the desolate Pine Ridge Reservation. Lakota Pony Rides hires local teens to guide groups of riders across the reservation land. The guides ensure that there is plenty of time for visitors to explore the reservation's terrain. White Plume says most people are surprised by what they see. He says they often make comments such as, "This is so beautiful and peaceful here. We never imagined it would be this way."[43] White Plume also uses his business to tell people about the Lakota heritage. He often takes riders on historical tours of the reservation, pointing out landmarks such as burial sites of important Lakota chiefs.

As Native Americans strive for economic self-sufficiency, they must adapt to new ways of life. These changes not only affect how people make a living, they also change the way people live from day to day.

Daily Life

Historically, Native American families had to rely on each other for survival. In many cases, families depended on other tribal members as well, creating strong bonds of kinship throughout the community. Today, the family in general and children in particular are still at the heart of the Native American society. Whether it is grandparents bringing grandchildren with them to a community fitness center or a village banding together to deal with a natural disaster, Native Americans feel close bonds with their family and neighbors and make a point of sharing their daily activities with the people they care about.

Aunties and Uncles

On many reservations, children live in extended families that include aunties, uncles, and cousins. "Aunties and uncles" are terms for adults who are not necessarily blood relatives but who play an important role in a child's life. Similarly, cousins are other young people on the reservation who may or may not be blood relatives. A teenager explains how these relationships are often formed at community gatherings, such as a powwow: "When you go to a powwow, you're surrounded by family, whether it's immediate family or extended.

A family of the Santa Clara pueblo in New Mexico gathers at their adobe home. Family serves as the focal point of Native American life.

And when you know someone for a long time, they begin to feel like family. You soon find yourself calling them auntie or grandma, or you introduce them as your cousin."[44]

Individuals feel an obligation to help take care of their extended tribal family, especially when someone is in need. For example, on many reservations there is a severe housing shortage. Native Americans, however, do their best to see that no tribal member is homeless. Hardly anyone will say no to a family member or friend who needs a place to stay. "Our tradition and culture tells us to watch out for one another,"[45] explains Ernie Little, executive director of Pine Ridge Reservation's housing agency. On many reservations, two, three, or even four families live together in a single-family home with mattresses on the floors and sofas serving as makeshift beds.

Many residents live in housing projects, known as clusters, that consist of a small group of homes without any nearby service facilities such as stores or gas stations. While the one-story single-family home is the most common type of housing on reservations, residents also live in trailer homes as well as in traditional housing, such as the adobe homes in the pueblos of New Mexico and the hogans of the Navajo people.

Many of the homes lack modern conveniences such as plumbing or kitchen facilities and do not have electricity or running water. Some residents use generators or gas-powered refrigerators, but many homes are simply one-room dwellings heated with a wooden stove and lit by kerosene lamps.

Many households have multiple generations living together. Grown children who are unable to buy homes of their own often return to their family home, bringing with them their spouses and children. On the Pine Ridge Reservation in South Dakora, for ex-

ample, the president of the Oglala Lakota Tribe shares his home with seventeen relatives, who include his daughter and son-in-law and their seven children.

Grandparents and Grandchildren

On many reservations grandparents and grandchildren live together, and grandparents are therefore active participants in the raising of their grandchildren. The relationship between grandparents and grandchildren has traditionally been a close one in most Native American societies. For hunting and gathering tribes, it was often more practical for the grandparents to take care of the grandchildren while the parents looked for food. The grandparents were responsible for passing their knowledge and wisdom to their grandchildren through instruction and stories.

The close relationship between grandparent and grandchild can still be found in tribal communities. Today, grandparents look after their grandchildren for a number of reasons. In some cases, the parents have to leave the reservation to find work; other times the parents are afflicted with illnesses that render them unable to care for their children. In such cases, the arrangement is supposed to be temporary. On the Pine Ridge Reservation in South Dakota, sixty-four-year-old Doris Eagle cared for seven of her grandchildren while their parents were going through an alcoholic treatment program. When the parents completed the program, they were reunited with their children.

Sometimes the parental relationship between grandparents and grandchildren becomes permanent, whether by necessity or by tradition. In some tribes, tradition dictates that grandparents raise their eldest grandchild.

Three generations of a Native American family are shown here. Extended families often live together on the reservation.

Both the Assiniboine and Gros Ventre tribes still follow this practice. The two tribes share the Fort Belknap Reservation in Montana, where nearly 30 percent of the families on the reservation are grandparents raising their grandchildren. Like other couples on the Fort Belknap Reservation, Mary Agnes and Joseph BlackCrow, members of the Assiniboin and Gros Ventre tribes, have adopted their eldest grandchild; in addition, they have adopted four other grandchildren.

Family Time

Even though Native American families enjoy being together, the isolation of most Indian reservations often means there is little time to spend in relaxing, fun activities with each other. For example, Derrith Watchman-Moore and her family live on the Navajo Reservation about thirty miles from Window Rock, Arizona, where Watchman-Moore works and where her two children attend school.

Navajo boys enjoy an after-school game of basketball. For many youngsters, the remoteness of reservation life means spending long hours away from home.

Much of their day is spent commuting between Window Rock and Crystal, the tiny town where they live in the remote Chuska Mountains.

The children get up at 5:15 A.M., which gives them about an hour to do chores, eat breakfast, and get dressed before having to leave for school. In the winter, when the roads are covered with ice and snow, the daily commute to town can take over an hour. When it snows, the family must use a tractor to clear the unpaved road from their home to the main road.

After their school day the children attend an after-school program where they wait for their mother to pick them up. Sometimes that can be as late as 6:30 P.M. By the time the family returns home, there is usually just enough time to eat dinner from a crock-pot before they need to get ready for bed.

Boys and Girls Clubs

Watchman-Moore's experience is typical in that her children finish school before she finishes work. Many Indian parents, then, must find a place for the children to go after school. On many reservations, the Boys and Girls Clubs of America (B&GCA) provide this vital service. The clubs work in partnership with tribes across the nation. There are more than 145 club locations in twenty-six states, serving sixty thousand Native American boys and girls. The clubs provide school-age youngsters a safe place after school. The children can get help with their homework, play games, or simply talk with their friends.

The clubs reflect the values and traditions of the communities in which they are located. Some offer cultural camps where children can learn their native language and traditions. The Boys and Girls Club of the Three Affili-ated Tribes on the Fort Berthold Reservation in North Dakota has a number of programs that feature storytelling, dancing, singing, and family night get-togethers. During the summer, about 140 young people participate in "Buffalo Pasture," a two-night, three-day event in the North Dakota Badlands, where the youngsters camp in tepees.

Some of the clubs focus on activities that teach children how to take care of animals. For example, the Boys and Girls Club of Aha Macay on the Fort Mojave Reservation in Arizona has a program where club members are responsible for eleven horses. Club members ride the horses on nearby trails and participate in horse shows and parades. During the summer months, the children arrive at the club's equestrian center early in the morning to help feed and groom the horses.

Many of the clubs provide state-of-the art facilities. The SuAnne Big Crow Boys and Girls Club on the Pine Ridge Reservation has a computer laboratory, classrooms, recreational facilities, a gym, and an Olympic-size swimming pool. It is the largest club on a reservation and serves five hundred children. The club is named in honor of SuAnne Big Crow, a popular and gifted high school basketball player who died in an automobile accident in 1992.

For many children the Boys and Girls Clubs are a more structured alternative to being at home. In some cases there is little supervision at home because parents are working and the grandparents are unavailable. In other cases, it can be difficult for children to study at home because their homes are overcrowded. Perhaps most important, the clubs provide a place for teens to gather in the absence of malls and libraries. In 2003 a Boys and Girls Club opened in Rough Rock, Arizona, on the Navajo Reservation. Rough Rock, like many reservation towns, has no malls, pizza parlors, bowling alleys, or libraries. Before the

Rough Rock club opened, a teenager who attended Rough Rock High School commented, "We really need to look into opening a Boys & Girls Club out here. There's really nothing here. [The students] just go home and kick back."[46]

Big Bat's

Like their children, most Native American adults appreciate the chance to hang out and meet each other. Often the local convenience store provides that opportunity. On the Pine Ridge Reservation, for example, Big Bat's, a convenience store near tribal headquarters, serves this function. When the owners of Big Bat's, Loren and Patty Pourier, opened the store in 1990, they offered residents amenities such as gas, groceries, and some fast food. But they quickly realized that the store had an even greater value to the reservation as a place for family and friends to spend time together. "People were hungry for someplace to congregate, to gather, to have a cup of coffee, to visit with old friends and to meet some new ones,"[47] says Loren Pourier.

Tribal elders often bring their *takojas*, or grandchildren, with them to the store. Oliver Red Cloud, a regular customer at Bat's, has this to say: "It's good for the kids. Before Big Bat's came, they used to just run around and get themselves in trouble. Now there's a place for them to go . . . to sit and talk and listen. There's a place for everyone to go, where the grandfathers and grandmothers can be with their takojas, and where everyone can learn from each other."[48]

Over the years, the Pouriers have made improvements to the store to help customers learn more about their culture. Inside the store, there is a 106-foot-long mural that depicts traditional stories of the Lakota Tribe, including the origin of the sacred pipe and the powwow.

Getting the News

While Big Bat's serves as a place for residents to learn about their heritage and exchange news, it is not practical for people to make a trip to the store every time they want to find out what is happening on the reservation. On Pine Ridge, as well as other reservations, residents get their news from a variety of sources, especially newspapers and radios.

On many reservations there are tribally owned newspapers, that provide information

Opera, Indian Style

Reservations offer limited entertainment choices. There are few movie theaters and even fewer venues that offer live entertainment. Even so, residents occasionally get the opportunity to see a play or in at least one instance, to watch an opera. In August 2001 opera professionals from New York and the Pacific Northwest staged a production of Mozart's opera, *The Magic Flute*, on the Kalispel Reservation in Washington.

The audience sat on blankets and lawn chairs for the one-day-only performance held on the tribal powwow grounds. It was the first time an opera had been performed on the reservation and included a narrator who spoke in English and Salish, the tribe's language. The Kalispel production included some Native American touches, such as the Frog Island drumming group, who appeared onstage in their regalia and sang in the chorus.

A Kaska Indian man of Canada's Yukon Territory works at a radio station. Residents of isolated reservations use radio to connect to the outside world.

about local events, tribal news from other reservations, and federal legislation that affects the entire Native American community. As an example, the *Sho-Ban News* is the weekly publication of the Shoshone-Bannock Tribes. The paper is read by about twenty-five hundred people living on the Fort Hall Reservation in Idaho. The *Sho-Ban News* reports on local and national events and includes coverage of community gatherings, job announcements, obituaries, school reports, and weather reports.

Prior to the 1980s and 1990s, however, when radio started replacing them, bulletin boards were the method residents used most to communicate with each other. The manager of the tribal radio station on the Hoopa Valley Reservation in California recalls what it was like before there was a radio station on the reservation: "Every store and just about every public wall around had cork board mounted somewhere. People would post their bulletins on different colors of paper that attract the eye. The wind would come up and blow and rustle them around."[49]

A Link to the World

On many reservations around the country, radio has replaced bulletin boards as the preferred way to communicate with other tribal members. For residents living in isolated areas, the radio has become an essential part of daily life because it helps to ease the sense of isolation. A writer in *Indian Country Today* comments: "The point here is that radio, in any rural area, is a direct link to the rest of the country—and to the world."[50]

Sometimes, radio provides residents with a sense of being connected to their own culture for the first time. For years, if residents on the Hopi Reservation wanted to listen to Native American programs, they tuned to the radio station broadcasting from the nearby Navajo Reservation. The only problem is that the station featured programs in the Navajo language, which most Hopi did not understand. In 2000 the Hopi tribe launched a radio station that allows Hopi to finally hear their native language over the airwaves. A reporter from the *New York Times*, who visited the Hopi when the new radio station opened, describes the ceremony:

> Standing before a microphone in the blazing sunlight on the station's front steps, Doran Dalton, the chairman of the Hopi Foundation, opened the first broadcast day of Indian country's newest radio station with a simple announcement: "You're listening to KUYI." Then Jimmy Lucero, a Hopi crier—every reservation village has one—stepped up to the microphone to shout the news, in Hopi.[51]

KILI

Radio stations that serve reservations differ from commercial stations in that instead of targeting a narrowly defined audience, they try to appeal to the broadest possible audience. In South Dakota, radio station KILI broadcasts over ten thousand square miles to residents on the Pine Ridge, Cheyenne River, and Rosebud reservations. On its Web site, KILI describes why people tune into the station:

> A grandmother in Medicine Root, South Dakota, awakens to the sounds of the Porcupine Singers A Lakota rancher from Kane Creek listens for the weather A young father in Wanblee waits to hear job announcements A young teenager in Kyle waits to hear rock and roll.[52]

KILI's programming day begins with a sunrise prayer followed by a Lakota language program. The station also has a health information roundup, a report from the local high school, job announcements, and local news and weather. In the evenings a live drum group performs.

Radio Programs

Because of the broad demographic range of their listeners, tribal stations offer a variety of local programming, including news and weather, funeral announcements, job announcements, and livestock and rodeo reports. Some stations provide programs to help preserve tribal languages, incorporating short vocabulary lessons into their broadcasts throughout the day.

Those who decide on a station's programming have the additional challenge of being sensitive to cultural taboos. For example, storytelling is a popular form of entertainment on many reservations. However, among some tribes, storytelling can only be done in the winter months. Radio stations broadcasting to these tribes must be sure that storytelling programs are only aired in the winter. If the programs were to run during some other time of the year, tribal members would consider it an insult because it goes against their cultural norms.

Some programs, however, have an almost universal appeal among Native Americans, whether on or off the reservation. By far the most popular show on most reservations is *Native America Calling*, a national live call-in talk show. The show brings together voices from Native communities throughout North America and has an audience of about two hundred thousand.

Native America Calling covers a wide range of topics including environmental issues, current events, and religion. Some of the broadcasts generate heated debates but not all the shows revolve around topical subjects. *Music Maker* is a regular monthly segment that highlights Native American musicians.

Over the years, radio shows such as *Native America Calling* have developed loyal listeners who go out of their way to make sure they do not miss any part of the program. In *Indian Country Today*, Dennis Newman, program director for a radio station on the Standing Rock Reservation in South Dakota, says that it is not uncommon for people driving on the reservations to turn their car around and drive in the direction they came from in order to continue listening to a radio program when the station signal becomes weak or when they know that no radio is available in the home they are going to visit.

Navajo Game Play

On the Navajo Nation Reservation, radio listeners can tune in to hear professional basketball play-by-play spoken in the Navajo language. During the basketball season, the tribal station broadcasts about three home games a month of the Phoenix Suns, a professional team based in Phoenix, Arizona.

Sports announcer L.A. (Laura Ann) Williams describes the action in both English and Navajo. Williams says the fast-paced nature of the games provides a challenge because Navajo is a detailed, precise language. Williams explains that traveling on the court is translated into Navajo as, "The player ran when he needed to dribble," and a breakaway is, "He's running really, really fast with the ball, and they're chasing him."

Radio Saves Lives

While the radio is an important source of entertainment and news, it plays a critical role during emergencies, such as massive wildfires that often break out during the summer and fall. Radio stations, like KNNB on the Fort Apache Reservation in central Arizona, provide services when a natural disaster puts lives and homes at risk. For example, for two weeks in June 2002, as fire engulfed the 1.6-million-acre reservation, KNNB expanded its broadcast hours an additional six hours a day and interrupted programs to update residents on areas that needed to be evacuated because they were threatened by the fire.

The reports were given in the Apache language, which helped to reassure the residents. "People were coming on the radio in Apache, giving information on the fire," said

Katy Aday, secretary in the tribal council office. "To hear it coming from our elders in Apache, it helped a lot."[53]

Stranded

Wildfires are just one of the natural hazards that residents must cope with. Flash floods and snowstorms are common on many reservations. When they hit, they can make roads completely impassable, cutting residents off from vital services. In February 1998 melting snow formed thick mud on the remote roads in the Navajo Nation, where Della Begay and her five elementary-school-age grandchildren live in an isolated area of the reservation. When the mud formed, Begay and the children found themselves stranded in their home.

After a few days, the Begays ran out of food and wood for their stove. They also did

Flooding and other natural dangers are common on reservations. This man looks at a storm-damaged road on the Makah Reservation in Washington.

not have any hay to feed to their livestock. To get new supplies, the Begays walked for four hours through deep snow and mud to reach a main dirt road five miles from their home. They then waited for three hours by the side of the road until they were able to get a lift to the Sawmill Chapter House. The chapter house serves as a temporary shelter during emergencies, providing cots for residents who cannot travel back and forth to their homes. When Begay and the children arrived at the chapter house, they warmed themselves by the woodstove and waited for the arrival of National Guard personnel, who helped the family return to their home with supplies of food and hay.

Long Drives

Even when natural disasters do not strike, it can be difficult for residents to obtain basic necessities. Most reservations offer little in the way of supermarkets, retail shops, or restaurants. For the most part, there are no shopping malls, banks, or hospitals on reservations. If residents need to buy furniture or make a bank deposit, they have to drive long distances to towns off the reservation. Even destinations located on the reservation can be far away. On the Wind River Reservation in central Wyoming, a community spread out over 9,100 square miles, towns may be thirty to forty miles apart.

Because of this lack of local amenities, the majority of people living on the reservation cannot get by without a car. Those residents who do not own cars must rely on others who are willing to share their vehicles. For this reason, when someone goes into town to church or some other social function, they will usually have a full carload of people. Because everyone knows everyone else on a reservation, drivers will often stop their cars and offer rides to people they see walking along the road.

Residents have to drive long distances to buy items such as groceries or clothing. When Julie Schindler spent a year teaching first grade on the Fort Belknap Reservation, Montana, she lived and worked in the tiny town of Hays, which has a post office, schools, two convenience stores, and a community center. Because the convenience stores offered only snacks and a few grocery items, Schindler had to make a monthly grocery-shopping trip to the nearest large town, which was Havre, Montana, located ninety miles away.

Trips like those made by Schindler are inconvenient, but living so far away from cities can be more than inconvenient; it can be life threatening to residents when a medical emergency arises. Individuals who are critically ill or seriously injured are transported to medical facilities on specially equipped planes or helicopters. On the Navajo Reservation, an air ambulance company takes patients to clinics on the reservation, or, if need be, to hospitals in larger cities in Arizona and New Mexico. The company makes about forty-five to fifty-five flights on the reservation each month.

Bus Systems

While helicopters serve the most serious medical cases, it is far more common for residents, especially the elderly, to put off routine care so that they can avoid driving on the reservation's dangerous roads. To alleviate this problem, a few tribal governments have invested in public transit systems. The buses cannot travel fast, as the routes can be long and involve many stops. On the Navajo Reservation, the Navajo Transit runs twenty-five

Mule Delivery

On the Supai Reservation in Arizona, mules used to deliver mail are often hampered by bad weather. Mules deliver everything from televisions to coffins to the reservation's three thousand residents, who live in a village at the bottom of the three-thousand-foot-deep Havasu Canyon.

Postmaster Charlie Chamberlain says that the greatest hazard of his job is flash floods, which hit without warning. In the October 1, 1999, article "Remote Tribe Gets Mail the Old Fashioned Way," Chamberlain tells a *Seminole Tribune* reporter: "I've been caught in a flash flood and once spent over three hours with all my mules on a ledge just wide enough for a man to stand. Once it's gone, you come back down off the ledge and deliver the mail."

A mailman and his mules cross a river on the Supai Reservation in Arizona. Because of the reservation's forbidding terrain, mules are used for deliveries.

buses and vans on seven fixed routes. Many of the routes are 100 miles or more one way. One of the routes is 160 miles and takes four hours to complete.

Other tribal bus systems are even more extensive. The Wind River bus system on the Wind River Reservation in Wyoming takes its fifteen thousand passengers a month to points on the reservation and beyond. The company offers on-demand service that will take riders as far as Salt Lake City, which is two hundred miles from the reservation. "We don't like to say 'no' to anyone because we are a general transit provider and we think if we refuse or deny a ride to just one person, then we're not doing our job," says one transit official. "We really go all out to provide whatever service the people need."[54]

The bus service can make a major difference in the everyday lives of reservation resi-dents, especially those with disabilities. In *Bus Ride Magazine* writer Frank Turco tells the story of a young man on the Wind River Reservation who became paralyzed shortly before he was to begin student teaching. The only way the student teacher could get to his assignment was in a vehicle equipped to handle wheel-chairs. The tribal bus system has such a vehicle and used it to transport the young man to his job. "We picked him up at his house with our bus every day, drove him to school and then drove him home again at night," says a transportation official. "That allowed him to graduate and succeed, and today he's a teacher."[55]

Because reservations are remote and isolated, residents rely on each other for their daily needs. But what makes them strong as a community are the beliefs, ceremonies, and celebrations that have been practiced for countless generations.

Beliefs, Ceremonies, and Celebrations

In Native American cultures prior to the establishment of the reservation system, religious rituals and ceremonies were a part of everyday life. Tribes performed these acts to help ensure the survival of the individuals in the community and the community as a whole. Native Americans believed that powerful, mysterious forces were responsible for maintaining life and these forces had to be acknowledged in order for the community to thrive. There were ceremonies to mark the important stages in a person's life, to cure illness, and to ensure a good harvest.

Fasting, drumming, singing, and dancing all played a part in these observances. After reservations were established, tribes were pressured by Christian missionaries and federal authorities to abandon their traditional rituals and ceremonies. In response, many Native Americans converted to Christianity, but they did not totally give up their traditional beliefs. Stanford Addison, an Arapaho elder on the Shoshone-Arapaho Reservation in Wyoming, explains that Native Americans adopted Christian rituals in order to placate the missionaries and allow at least some forms of native worship to be preserved.

Over the years the federal government changed its policy toward native spiritualism, and in 1978 Congress passed the American Indian Religious Freedom Act, which gave tribes the right to practice their traditional religions. The ceremonies performed today are not the same as those performed hundreds of years ago, as they have changed to reflect the way Native Americans live now. In some cases, the ceremonies are held to help solve modern-day problems, and in other cases they include nontraditional elements, such as Christian prayers and songs.

Sunrise Rituals

Many Native Americans begin their day with a morning ritual, which often includes singing and praying. In Montana, members of the Cheyenne Tribe perform a purifying ceremony, in which individuals step up to a cluster of burning sweetgrass and pull the smoke toward them with four scooping motions. Anthony Littlewhirlwind, a member of the tribe, explains the purpose of the ritual. "Sometimes we need to purify the mind, clean the mind from bad thoughts and clean the heart of bad feelings,"[56] he says.

On some reservations, such as Navajo Nation, residents say a traditional prayer when the sun first appears in the sky. In the *Arizona Republic*, reporter Betty Reid writes about the sunrise ceremony that her mother, Dorothy, performs in the morning at her home in Navajo Nation. Dorothy is in her seventies and lives in a small hogan, a traditional Navajo house. Reid describes her mother's daily routine, which begins when she gives thanks to the deities: "It's not yet 4 A.M. and my mother is already stirring. By the light of the [kerosene] lamp, my mother limps across the uneven floor and out the front door to perform her morning prayer ritual to the Dawn People. She holds up a fistful of white cornmeal and lets it sprinkle slowly through her fingers so that the Navajo gods will bless the day."[57]

There are people who still follow the tradition of a morning prayer like Betty Reid's mother does, but do not use traditional prayers. For example, in Montana, on the Fort Belknap Reservation, Mary Agnes BlackCrow was taught to give thanks in the morning. "My grandparents always told me before you do anything, you pray,"[58] she says. However, instead of the deity her forebears worshipped, BlackCrow uses rosary beads and says her prayer in English, addressing God as Catholics have traditionally done.

Pueblo Dances

In the pueblos, or villages, in northern New Mexico, residents hold dance ceremonies that combine southwestern native ceremonies and

Religious rituals are a part of daily life for many Native Americans. Pictured is a traditional ceremony of purification and ground blessing.

Dancers perform the Matachines Dance at San Ildefonso Pueblo in New Mexico.
This ceremonial dance is performed various times throughout the year.

Spanish-introduced Catholic celebrations. The dances are performed in pueblo kivas, ceremonial chambers built into the ground. The dances, which celebrate the bounty of Mother Earth, are performed throughout the year. Exactly which dance residents perform depends upon the season. In the spring the dancers pray for good crops, and in the autumn the dancers celebrate the harvest. In the winter the dancers dress as buffalo and deer in appreciation of the animals that give up their lives so that people may live.

Dances are also performed for Catholic saints' days and Christian holidays. A writer who attended the Christmas Eve dance at Nambe, a pueblo with 650 residents, filed the following eyewitness report:

> The buffalo come out to dance by the light of a great bonfire. They come after evening Mass at the ancient St. Francis of Assisi church, and dance for just a little while before returning to the kiva, the underground ceremonial chamber, center of the pueblo's traditional religious life. With the buffalo come the deer, their horns cir-

cled with sprigs of fir, like candles in Advent wreaths, the antelope and a couple of Pueblo Indians dressed up as their old enemies, the Comanches, for comic relief.[59]

Native American Church

While the Catholic Church has a strong presence on reservations, the Native American Church of North America has a large following. The church was started by Native Americans in 1918 and blends the teachings of Christianity with native spiritualism. Church membership is estimated at 250,000. Churches can be found on seventy reserva-

tions, mostly in the West. In recent years the church has grown the most rapidly on the Navajo Reservation.

Church ceremonies include the ritual use of peyote, a mildly hallucinogenic cactus. The peyote, which has long been held as a sacred medicine by some tribes, is a small, spineless cactus native to southern Texas and north-central Mexico. Members of the Native American Church believe that ingesting small amounts of peyote helps them receive spiritual knowledge.

The church does not have professionally trained clergy. Instead, members are encouraged to read and interpret the Bible on their own. The church teaches its followers to be faithful to their spouses, refrain from drinking alcohol, and show respect for the earth. The church service is informal and includes Native American elements. In Huston Smith's book *One Nation Under God*, Jay Fikes writes about a typical Native American Church service:

> Singing occupies about sixty percent of the Church's devotional ritual. Each of about twenty-five worshipers has ample opportunity to sing to the accompaniment of a gourd rattle and small drum that is pounded rapidly. Singing is often in the local Native American language, but English phrases like "Jesus only" and "He's the Savior" are likely to erupt. Worshipers sing, drum, pray, meditate, and consume peyote during all-night meetings.[60]

Tobacco

Native Americans believe that certain substances, such as peyote and tobacco, have spiritual powers. Tribes use tobacco as a medicine

These pots contain peyote cactus, a plant used in worship ceremonies in the Native American Church of North America.

and in religious ceremonies. It plays a key role in the Sacred Pipe Ceremony, one of the most important Native American ceremonies. During the ceremony, participants sit in a circle, passing around a lit pipe filled with tobacco. As the pipe is passed to each person in turn, the individual says a prayer and the smoke rising from the pipe represents a visible expression of the prayer.

Tobacco is also used as an offering to spiritual guardians, beings who are believed to have powers to give people good health, success, and help during a crisis. On some reservations individuals try to use the power of tobacco to give them an advantage in a dis-

pute, such as those that are heard in tribal courts. For example, in April 2001 the Medill News Service reported: "In the Muscogee (Creek) Nation tribal court, a medicine man may visit and sprinkle tobacco around the courtroom, purporting to be able to put hexes on people in an effort to further his cause."[61]

Tobacco is also used in courtrooms as part of the swearing-in process where witnesses promise to tell the truth. Those giving testimony sometimes take an oath to tell the truth by putting their hand over the Bible, but they may also take their oath over tobacco leaves. A tribal judge explains that because tobacco has a religious significance to Native Americans, "Indian people are not going to lie if they put tobacco out."[62]

Tobacco is also sometimes given to tribal elders in exchange for their counsel and wisdom. During the summer of 2001, a journalism student from the University of California at Berkeley visiting the Shoshone-Arapaho Reservation in Wyoming was told she should bring tobacco with her when she met Stanford Addison, a tribal elder. On the way to Addison's home, the student stopped at a convenience store on the reservation to buy a pack of cigarettes. Once she reached her destination, the student produced the pack of cigarettes, which Addison took without saying a word.

Sweat Lodge

The sweat lodge is used in a traditional ceremony that allows people to get in touch with the spiritual world. The sweat lodge ceremony serves as an opportunity for teaching, praying, and singing. It is thought to bring both spiritual and physical health.

There are several different types of sweat lodges, but the most common is a small round hut, about three to four feet high and five to six feet in diameter. The hut is covered with wood and branches and has an outermost layer consisting of leather or buckskin, which helps retain the heat. In the center of the hut is a hole filled with fire-heated stones. The

Pictured is the framework for a sweat lodge, which will be covered with leather and buckskin. Native Americans hold traditional ceremonies in these to connect with the spiritual world.

room's temperature is controlled by pouring water from a dipper onto the stones to create steam.

The dippers of water that participants draw from the bucket represent their requests for prayers. On some reservations in the Northwest, it is customary for participants to draw a picture of a cross on the ground with the water. The cross, according to Arapaho elder Stanley Addison, "represents the coming of the Bible, because when we're in that sweat we're not there to discriminate

against prayer. All these ways are the ways of the Creator."[63] Participants say that the sweat lodge makes their praying more intense.

During the sweat, participants sometimes pass around the tribal pipe and ask the deities for courage and strength. In the *Wall Street Journal*, reporter Jonathan Eig wrote about a sweat lodge ceremony that took place on the Pine Ridge Reservation in South Dakota:

> The wind howled and snow lashed across the plain, but inside the small insulated hut, Bryan Brewer was soaked in sweat. Almost every week, he and a dozen other men, most of them professional educators, come to a barren field on the Pine Ridge Indian Reservation to take part in a Native American ritual. As he sat in the dark of the sweat lodge and stared into a pit full of glowing rocks, Mr. Brewer prayed. He prayed in English and in Sioux—for his family, for his community and for Pine Ridge High School, where he recently and somewhat reluctantly became principal.[64]

Traditional Healing

While American Indians use modern medicine, some people prefer traditional healers. These healers gather plants and foods found on the reservation, which have been used for thousands of years to cure illnesses and ailments. Examples of medicinal plants include milkweed, which treats arthritis, and chokecherries, which stop diarrhea. Natural healers say that modern medicine only treats the physical body while traditional medicine focuses on the mind and soul.

Wilbert Fish, a medicine man on the Blackfeet Reservation in Montana is often asked to treat his fellow tribal members. When the reservation had a flu outbreak, Fish worked day and night to prepare two hundred gallons of a traditional treatment. In the *Indian Country Today* article "Slice of Buffalo Lung Beats Potato Chips Any Day," Fish is quoted as saying that patients are usually referred to him when modern medicine has been unable to help someone. "The sad thing is that people don't come to medicine men until they're almost dead," he says.

Vision Quest

The vision quest is another traditional ceremony that provides spiritual guidance during difficult times. People go on a vision quest to seek an answer to a problem or to help discover what their path in life should be. At one time, the vision quest was a part of nearly every Native American youth's experience.

The quest usually lasts for three to four days, during which time the individual stays in a remote area without food or water. As the person fasts and prays, he or she often experiences visions or dreams, in which a spirit guide provides a solution to the problem or predicts the future.

On the the Pine Ridge Reservation, Rita Little Boy went on a vision quest when she and her husband, Michael, faced an obstacle to getting a new home. The Little Boys wanted to replace the one-room house they shared with their seven children but were told by the Pine Ridge housing authority that they did not qualify for a new home.

During her quest Rita fasted and prayed. She also had a dream in which a very old man appeared and told her, "when the grass turns green what you asked for will be waiting for you."[65] A short while later, when the weather became warmer and grass was green, the Little Boys received a new home from an organization that provides surplus military mobile homes to reservation families.

Naming Ceremony

Like the vision quest, the naming ceremony was once a rite of passage for most Native American children. The ceremony had all but disappeared on many reservations but has been revived in recent years. In 2001 the Loneman School on the Pine Ridge Reservation held a naming ceremony, the first time in the school's history that it had sponsored such an event. Parents and teachers gave a great deal of thought to choosing the right names. Sometimes they chose a name that reflected the way the child was at the time of the ceremony, and for others they chose a name that the child could grow into. "As a Lakota, the quest of the identity is a measure of how you're going to be as a man or woman some day in the future,"[66] says a Loneman teacher. About one hundred people attended the 2001 naming ceremony, which included a Lakota drum, a prayer offering, and a blessing by a spiritual leader. At the ceremony the children were given names such as Stand Among Horses, Afraid of His Horses, Golden Boy, Sun Sees All People Woman, and White River Woman.

Powwows

The biggest social event on most reservations is the tribe's annual powwow. The powwow is an event that serves as a celebration, dance competition, social gathering, and reunion all rolled into one. The powwow is not just a place to dance or eat, however, for as one writer explains:

> The powwow is a time for renewing and revisiting; a time to gather and dance, sing, visit with old friends and make new ones.
>
> It is a living thing, and by participating, tribes and their members actively preserve a rich cultural tradition.
>
> More than a social event, the powwow works as an anchor to tribal ideas, attitudes and values. Because of its importance to both individuals and groups, the powwow is an enduring ritual.[67]

Although in the past the powwow was a celebration of local tribal customs, today it is a multicultural event that brings tribes from across North America together to celebrate simply being Native American. For both the dancers and audience, the powwow is a religious ceremony. As a writer in the *Wind River News* wrote: "But as with the sacred thread that runs through all of life, there are sacred traditions to be found in this coming together of people."[68]

Powwows can be large or small. Some powwows are annual events attended by large

Wearing traditional dress, Shoshone girls dance in a powwow. The powwow is a ceremony that brings together tribes from all over the continent.

numbers of people from one tribe or even from many different tribes. Other powwows are held for special occasions, such as celebrating a graduation or the birth of a baby. Sometimes family members and friends hold a powwow to honor someone important in their lives, such as a tribal elder.

Powwows are often held when tribal high schools win athletic events, such as state basketball championships. For example, in 2002 four teams from reservations in Montana swept the state finals. The teams from the Fort Belknap and Blackfeet reservations clinched the titles of state champs in their division when they beat teams from the Fort Peck and Flathead reservations. Fans of the teams threw parades and powwows to honor the athletes and celebrate their victories.

The Gathering of Nations

While most powwows are held for one specific purpose, the largest powwow, known as the Gathering of Nations, is designed to promote the traditions and culture of Native

American people generally. The gathering, which is held every April at the University of New Mexico in Albuquerque, brings together over three thousand Native American dancers and singers representing five hundred North American tribes, including the Cherokee of Oklahoma, the Alabama-Coushatta of Texas, and the Puyallup of Washington State. The event includes an Indian traders market with eight hundred participating artists and a Miss Indian World beauty contest.

Most powwows are much smaller than the Gathering of Nations. Still, preparations for a powwow start months before the event. Organizers are responsible for making sure there is a drum group, an emcee, dance judges, and food and merchandise vendors. The vendors sell items related to or made by Native Americans, such as jewelry, flutes, baskets, pottery, and blankets.

Typical powwow food includes fry bread, Indian tacos, and hamburgers. Fry bread is deep-fried dough, similar to a doughnut. To make an Indian taco, the fry bread is topped with ground beef, pinto beans, shredded lettuce, shredded American cheese, diced tomatoes, and diced onions. Lemonade and soda pop are commonly sold at powwows. Alcohol, because of its long history of destructiveness in Indian communities, is not permitted at powwows.

The Grand Entry

Powwows can be held indoors or outdoors. Rows of bleachers or chairs form the dance circle. In the center is the dance arena, known as the arbor. Before the powwow a spiritual leader blesses the arbor. The blessing honors Mother Earth, Father Sky, and the air around. There also are songs to honor the men and women who have served in the armed forces. At the start of the powwow military veterans carrying flags enter the arena first, followed by the other dancers in a ceremony known as the Grand Entry. The inclusion of military veterans in this part of the celebration is an acknowledgment of the

Disabled Powwow Dancer Inspires Others

The fact that Conway Thompson is disabled with muscular dystrophy and needs to use a wheelchair has not stopped the teenager from becoming a dancer on the powwow circuit. Conway, who is a tribal member of the Cheyenne River Sioux in South Dakota, began dancing in 1998.

In the article "Just Keep Dancing" that appeared in *News from Indian Country*, Conway's mother, Kay, tells how Conway started dancing. "He saw everyone else dancing and just decided that he wanted to try it. He said, 'Hey, I can do that, too.' He's been going ever since."

Conway does his dancing in a powered wheelchair that allows him to stop on a dime, reverse direction, and spin in circles. "I just get dizzy once in a while," he says. Conway is well known throughout the American Indian community, and in 2003 the Rapid City's Black Hills Powwow honored him at a special celebration.

"He's amazing," said Marcy Gray, a representative for West Med Rehab of Rapid City, South Dakota. "He's living his culture, and so many people don't . . . they sit on the sidelines. But he's showing them that they can. He's doing things that adults aren't even doing. It's great."

community's respect for those who exhibit bravery as warriors, in this case by their service in the armed forces.

Even though the powwow provides a casual atmosphere for family and friends to gather together, there are certain rules that attendees are expected to follow. The *Wind River News*, the newspaper on the Wind River Reservation, posted some of these rules:

When the eagle staff is brought in during the Grand Entry, everyone stands. Hats are removed in respect. That same respect is shown should an eagle feather fall during the dancing. Everything must stop until a proper returning of the feather has been performed.

Pointing a finger, particularly the index finger, is considered impolite. It's best to indicate a person or direction by pursing the lips and pointing the eyes or to nod in the direction. For the Lakota, indicating with the thumb or little finger, while not preferred, would still be more polite than pointing the index finger, but never toward a person.

As with most events involving competition and concentration, camera flashes can be distracting. . . . Ask permission before snapping an individual's photograph outside the dancing, for this is private time.

Don't bother performers or stand in front of those preparing to dance or those singing.

Don't touch any costumes. Ornaments and many of the handmade outfits have special meanings, and also cost thousands of dollars, are cherished, and sometimes are made by a respected family member. Frequently they are heirlooms and may be delicate.

Feel free to join in the intertribal dances by invitation of the Master of Ceremonies.[69]

Keeping the Beat

The focal point of the powwow is the dancing. The drum group sits next to the dance arena, keeping the beat for the dancers, who dance in the center section. The drum circle is an important part of the festivities. In *Alberta Sweetgrass* Ethel Winnipeg writes, "Drummers are the heartbeat of the powwow. If there weren't any drummers, what would the dancers dance to?"[70] Songs can be either contemporary or traditional and often tell about everyday life, such as family, joy, and mourning.

The larger powwows usually offer dancers a cash prize, which can be as high as one thousand dollars. There are even some dancers who travel from reservation to reservation to compete in dance competitions. Some powwow dancers travel as much as thirty thousand miles across the United States and Canada each year, going from powwow to powwow.

There are several different types of dances used at powwows, such as the Omaha style of grass dancing and the Ojibwa style of jingle dress dancing. The traditional dance categories usually require dancers to keep the beat of the music while standing in one place or moving slowly in a circle. The fancy dance category is more lively and allows dancers to use faster and more intricate dance steps.

Each type of dance also requires certain outfits, known as regalia. In the traditional

Powwow dance outfits are known as regalia. The outfits are often handed down from one generation to the next. Regalia reflects the personality of the dancer. In some cases, the outfit tells the story of how the dancer got his or her Indian name.

Making the regalia can be a time-consuming process. It can take up to eight months to make a buckskin dress. In an article entitled "Siletz Beader Uses Craft to Help Youth," appearing in *Indian Country Today*, reporter Cate Montana writes about how one Native American woman goes about making a dress:

"It takes one giant elk hide, about 19 to 21 square feet, for a woman's dress and a 12- to 15-square-foot elk hide for a young girl's dress. Each one requires three to four deer hides to be cut into strips for fringe and a couple of thousand shells, pine nuts and beads for decoration. The shells and pine nuts may either be gathered by hand, ground and prepared for use, or purchased from a supply house. Each shell, nut, and bead is individually applied and basket wrapped."

Each bead, feather, and shell on this Native American's regalia has been painstakingly applied by hand.

dance category, women wear traditional buckskin dresses with elaborate beadwork. Women who dance in the fancy shawl category wear colorful shawls, which they incorporate into their dances. Traditional male dancers usually wear either cloth or skin leggings and a breech cloth decorated with ribbons and beadwork. For the men's fancy feather dance, the dancers' outfits include two bustles of either turkey or eagle feathers.

Young people learn the dance steps in a number of ways. Often a parent or older sibling will teach a child. In other cases children attend after-school programs that offer classes in dancing. But some youngsters are able to figure it out on their own. One teenage powwow dancer said he learned how to dance by watching other people and then adding his own style to it.

Teenage Dancers

Powwows play an important role in the lives of Native American teens and provide an outlet for dancing and meeting others. During

Beliefs, Ceremonies, and Celebrations

These canoeists paddling in a bay on Washington's Tulalip Reservation are participating in a multitribal celebration called the Canoe Journey.

the summer, when they are free from school obligations, the young people follow the powwow trail, dancing in powwows on different reservations.

The powwows teach the young people about respect, honor, and Native American pride. A teenager who danced at summer powwows wrote about how the drumming and singing at powwows made her feel connected to her culture: "Many of my peers love rap music. While I like country, and even a little rap, the songs I hear in my head—the ones I want to listen to repeatedly—are powwow songs."[71]

Canoe Journey

In the Pacific Northwest young Native Americans can get in their canoes and retrace an-

cient water routes used by their ancestors. The Canoe Journey is a multitribal festival that features a two-week canoe trip along the coastal waters of Washington State followed by a one-week celebration on the host tribe's reservation. Participants on the canoe journey range in age from seven to seventy.

In 2003 the Tulalips sponsored the journey, which had sixty canoes from forty tribes. Participating tribes included the Muckleshoot, the Suquamish, and the Swinomish-Samish. Most of the tribes were from the coastal area, but some came from inland locations. The canoes varied in size with some able to accommodate a dozen paddlers and others just big enough for four people.

For many participants the canoe journey is the first time they have paddled routes that Native Americans once used to trade goods and supplies. To complete the difficult journey tribes must help one another as they encounter thick fog, high winds, and ocean swells. On the first day of the event the tribal canoe from the Snoqualmie Reservation east of Seattle capsized but was quickly rescued by the Quinalt tribal canoe.

Fighting the ocean currents means long, hard days of paddling, but that does not stop the participants from socializing at the end of the day after setting up camp. "With the canoe journey you forget about time and sched-ules," said one participant. "Everyone becomes part of the canoe family."[72]

At the end of the canoe journey there is a large celebration that includes singing, dancing, and drumming. Thousands of people come to watch the paddlers come ashore in a procession led by the canoe of the host tribe.

Although the country's tribes have different customs, beliefs, and rituals, the tribes share a common goal to pass their cultural traditions to the next generation to ensure that the old ways do not die.

Cultural Preservation

For generations American Indians followed the customs, traditions, and practices that had been passed down to them from their ancestors. But much of this knowledge was lost when the reservation system was created. The federal government took children from their homes and sent them to boarding schools where only English was spoken and where children were punished for speaking their native language. Some of the children never returned to the reservation, but many of those who did had forgotten their culture and were not able to speak their native language. Furthermore, removed from their homes and distanced from their relatives, Native American children lost the opportunity to learn their traditions from the tribal elders.

Cultural Preservation Officers

In the last few decades Native Americans have been working through tribal cultural preservation officers to recover from this loss. The cultural preservation officer works to restore, preserve, and retain the tribe's traditions and culture. The preservation officer researches, archives, protects, and conserves traditional and natural resources on the reservation and works with other groups, such as the National Park Service, to develop programs that preserve the tribe's cultural heritage.

Cultural preservation covers nearly all aspects of a tribe's identity, including origins, histories, and stories; traditions, values, and beliefs; language, song, and dance. The officer also ensures the mental, physical, and spiritual well-being of tribal members. Since Native American culture values and respects the natural environment, cultural preservation also includes the uses of land areas, waterways, animal life, marine life, and plant life.

Reviving Dying Languages

One of the most pressing needs in the Native American community is developing programs to preserve native languages. Tribal languages are dying out at a rate that Native Americans find alarming. It is estimated that if current trends continue, 80 to 90 percent of the 175 existing native languages in the United States could become extinct within the next generation.

The loss of a language represents a loss of culture as well, for words reflect what is important to a people and how they see the world around them. Native Americans believe that if their languages continue to die, they will completely lose their identity as Native Americans. As one educator at a Montana tribal college expressed, "If we don't know the language, we probably won't be Indian people anymore. We'd be Americans with nice tans."[73]

One reason that Native American languages are dying out is that English is the language in which business is conducted on most reservations. It is used at tribal government functions, such as council meetings and courts. English is the first language for most children, who speak it at home and at school. With so little exposure to fluent speakers in their native languages, children rarely become fluent speakers themselves. In most cases, children learn a few words or phrases in their native language but not much more. Teenagers on reservations often speak a slang dialect of their language that uses simple words and phrases. There are exceptions. For example, on the Miccosukee Reservation in southern Florida, children speak the Miccosukee language at home and learn English at the tribal school.

A Lost Art

Women of the Eastern Shoshone Tribe on the Wind River Reservation in Wyoming are taking a step back in time to learn traditional basket weaving, an art form that still thrives on other reservations but has disappeared on the Wind River Reservation. Traditional baskets were made from red willow, milkweed, cattail, and cottonwood suckers. The baskets had a variety of purposes, including carrying and storing food.

Margaret Mathewson, an ethnobotanist from Oregon, gave basket-weaving classes at the Shoshone Cultural Center on the reservation. In the article "Traditional Shoshone Art of Basket Weaving Revived" in the *Wind River News*, reporter Jennifer Hafner recorded the comments from the participants as they struggled to make their baskets. "It's difficult to learn," said Pat Bergie. "We're having a tough time."

The tribe is hoping to have other Native Americans come to the cultural center to demonstrate more weaving techniques. "A long time ago we did this," said Noreen Panzetanga of Fort Washakie. "It seems like it should have been carried on, but it got lost somewhere."

A basket maker teaches children to weave baskets. Basketry was once a common skill on the Wind River Reservation of Wyoming.

Although many Native American languages are in danger of dying as the older tribal members who speak them die, many words live on in the English language. Many place names are derived from Native American words, such as Canada, Mississippi, Nebraska, and Oklahoma. Other Native American words that are part of everyday English include caribou, chipmunk, moose, squash, skunk, and toboggan, to name just a few.

This view of the Florida Everglades is from the Pa-Hay-Okee boardwalk. The term means "grassy water" in the Miccosukee language.

Navajo Speakers

There are reservations that still have a large number of native language speakers, but they are generally older residents. On the Navajo Nation Reservation many of the elderly residents who live in remote areas of the reservation speak only Navajo. These individuals often have a difficult time communicating with others on the reservation. In many cases, medical workers, especially doctors, speak English only. Fearing that the language barrier was keeping Navajo elderly from seeking medical help, the tribal health care services recently trained twenty-three people to become medical interpreters. The interpreters must speak Navajo fluently and attend training sessions to learn medical terminology.

While the large number of fluent speakers of the Navajo language ensures that the language will not become extinct soon, this is not the case on most reservations. Far more typical is the situation found on the Yerington Reservation in Nevada, where only a handful of people can still speak the language. "We have five elders fluent in the Yerington dialect. They're all 75 or older. Once they're gone, there will be no more Yerington dialect,"[74] says a tribal member.

In general, then, language preservation involves encouraging younger people to become fluent in the language of their ancestors. To accomplish this, tribes are sponsoring language programs that start before the children enter kindergarten. Tribal elders of the Upper Sioux Community in Minnesota, for example, spend part of their day in a preschool, speaking the Dakota language to the children. Once a week, for the families of the students, the school hosts a potluck dinner where bingo and other games are played using Dakota as well.

In South Dakota, a tribal college offers a day care center where the children speak only the Dakota language. At the Siceca Learning Center on the campus of the Sisseton Wahpeton College, the preschoolers learn to sing familiar songs, such as "London Bridge Is Falling Down," in Dakota. Teaching the language to children is complicated by the fact that Dakota spoken by men is different from that spoken by women. Therefore, both men and women elders visit the center so that the children who attend will hear both dialects.

Immersion Schools

When students enter school, some benefit from attending immersion schools, where only their native language is spoken. In upstate New York the Mohawks have a language-immersion school where students speak only Mohawk until their last two years, when they are given classes in English. The Akwesasne Freedom School is one of about fifty such immersion schools in the country. The school aims to increase the number of native speakers on the St. Regis Mohawk

Reservation, where there are about two to three thousand native language speakers out of roughly twelve thousand people.

Educators on the Blackfeet Reservation in Montana are using the immersion method to produce the first young fluent speakers of Piegan, the Blackfeet language, in a generation. At the Nizipuhwahsin Center, for children in kindergarten through eighth grade, English is a second language. All classes are conducted in Piegan. The idea, says a teacher at the school, is for children to either "sink or swim" in learning their native language.

According to Blackfeet tribal members, the students attending the Nizipuhwahsin Center will hold a special place within the tribe: "Any Blackfeet who will be able to speak our language fluently in 2005 will be indeed an outstanding and respected individual because it will be very rare to find such an individual."[75] Tribal members are optimistic that the program will keep the Piegan language alive. A mother of several students at the center expressed her thoughts: "The greatest thing about this school is that my children, including all the kids at the Nizipuhwahsin Center, are bringing the language into the next century," she said. "Now it won't die."[76]

It is still too early to tell if attempts to create fluent speakers will work or not. The biggest test will be to see if the children growing up today are comfortable enough with their language to use it in their homes and teach it to their children.

Dictionaries

One of the greatest challenges in teaching native languages is that most of the languages have never been written down. Even so, some people are working at compiling

A student writes on the board at an immersion school where class is held in the Blackfoot language. The immersion school helps keep the tribe's language alive.

dictionaries that offer English translations of native words. On the Flathead Reservation in Idaho, Drusilla Gould, a Lemhi-Shoshone woman, is creating a Shoshone dictionary. Shoshone, like most other Native American languages, is an oral language. Gould said the only evidence of the Shoshone language having ever been written is some markings on stones in Canada.

Gould notes that part of the difficulty in producing a dictionary is that there are cultural differences as well as language differences. For instance, there are no Shoshone words for hello or goodbye. She explains, "To use 'goodbye' would mean forever. We always say 'I will see you later' or 'I expect to see you

later.'" She also says that there are no swear words in Shoshone because "we are taught to be careful of what we say. We can heal people with words. We can make people ill with words."[77]

History Detectives

While the immersion schools and dictionaries are aimed at keeping languages alive for future generations, many tribes look to the past and sponsor programs that record and preserve tribal history. Preservation officers often act as detectives as they research and investigate leads about the history of the tribe and its members. The officers find this information in a number of ways, such as interviewing tribal elders, reviewing historical documents, and conducting archaeological digs. In recent years the officers have also used the Internet to track down individuals who might have important information about the tribe or items related to the tribe's history.

In Montana the Crow Place Name Project is helping to create a link between the land and the tribe's history. As part of the project, tribal elders are recalling the traditional Crow names for the places and sites on the Crow Reservation. Although the locations now have English names on maps created by the state of Montana, tribal elder Barney Old

Coyote remembers the names his people have used for thousands of years. An article in *Indian Country Today* recounts Old Coyote's memories: "When Barney Old Coyote looks across his homeland in Crow reservation, he can point to places like Anmaalapammuua, 'Where the Whole Camp Mourned,' Baahpalohkahpe, the place where the Crows first celebrated the Fourth of July, and Bisshiilannuusaau, 'Where They Laid Down Yellow Blankets.'"[78]

Old Coyote and other tribal elders are working with instructors from Little Big Horn College to document the place names and explain their meaning. As an example, the name Anmaalapammuua, "Where the Whole Camp

Code Talkers

Native American languages played an important role in the United States winning key battles in World War I and World War II. Comanche, Hopi, Choctaw, and Navajo tribal members acted as code talkers, communicating vital information in their native languages. Because these languages were only spoken and had never been written down, the languages served as an undecipherable code that the enemy was unable to break. The code talkers have received many awards in recognition of their service and often have powwows held in their honor.

During World War II, code talkers like this man relayed crucial information in their native tongues, which were unintelligible to the enemy.

Mourned," refers to the site where a war party returned to the tribe after suffering many casualties at a place called Rainy Buttes. Old Coyote says so many warriors were killed that not one family was unaffected, and everyone was in mourning. The project has recorded five hundred locations on the 2.2-million-acre Crow Reservation as well as other sites in North America.

Hopi Oral History Project

Just as the Crow elders were asked to provide important information about place names, tribal elders on other reservations have been involved in projects to record their knowledge about traditional culture, such as art and music, as well as the influence that reservations have had on tribal life. In Arizona the Hopi preservation officer is asking tribal elders to participate in the Hopi Oral History Project, which is gathering stories about different aspects of life on the Hopi Reservation since its inception.

The Hopi Oral History Project is designed to document the changes in traditions that have occurred in the tribe since the reservation era. Specifically it is looking for information about life in the Hopi villages in the late nineteenth century and early twentieth century. The preservation officer is interviewing the elderly residents to find out how different events, such as war and land disputes, affected individual villages. The tribe is interested in learning about a number of different topics, including the first Hopi tribal council; the Depression years of the 1930s; churches on the reservation; Hopi employment with the U.S. Forest Service and the Santa Fe Railroad; reservation trading posts; and sheep herding and animal husbandry.

Archaeological Clues

In addition to recording tribal history, the cultural officer works to preserve items of historical significance. When new buildings are constructed on the reservations, the officer makes sure that they are not built over archaeologically significant sites and that artifacts are preserved. Tribes want to ensure that artifacts such as tools, weapons, clothing, and containers are identified and retained by the tribes. These items often offer important clues about the lives of Native Americans before European settlers arrived.

When the tribal officials on the Salt River Reservation in Arizona wanted to build a new tribal complex, they hired an archaeological firm to test the proposed construction site looking for ancient ruins. The firm dug long trenches and then inspected the sides of the trenches, looking for artifacts, charcoal stains caused by fire, and other clues of human activity.

This procedure resulted in the discovery of a seven-hundred-year-old structure known as a pit house. The house was part of a village that had been inhabited by a group of people called the Hohokam. The house provided information about the way that the Hohokam constructed their homes and the material they used to make pottery. Although the pit house helped researchers understand the people who had lived there hundreds of years before, the tribe decided to build the new complex over the pit house because the site had already been damaged from construction of the tribal rodeo grounds in the 1950s.

Oneida Digs

On the Oneida Nation's reservation in New York, tribal officials enlist young people to

Archaeologists excavate Hopi ruins in Arizona. Archaeological digs yield ancient tribal artifacts, which shed light on tribal history and customs.

help archaeologists find tribal artifacts dating back three to four hundred years. For several years Oneida teens worked alongside archaeology professors and students from Colgate University. About seventy Oneida teens participated in the program, which helped piece together the history of the Oneida people.

The work on the archaeological digs was detailed and tedious. The students spent most of their time sifting soil through small-mesh screens to separate dirt from tiny artifacts like pottery fragments. The soil they were sifting most likely came from a trash pit. Because the pieces were often very tiny, the students had to train their eyes to learn what to look for. In all, the group found thousands of items, including glass trade beads, gun parts, bone fragments, and bits of traditional food such as maize, beans, and squash.

The team also dug test pits, which led to the discovery of a longhouse, a wooden structure that was big enough for all the members of an extended family to live together. The location of the longhouse on a hill overlooking a

A priest officiates at a reburial ceremony of an Eyak Indian in Alaska. Many tribes are working to recover ancestral remains that are housed in museums.

valley confirmed tribal lore that had been handed down for generations. "We have our stories. We have our legends," said an Oneida official. "We have nothing physical to go with our stories and legends. We know we've been here for thousands of years, but to know there was a long house goes along with our stories. They're not myths."[79]

Once the researchers at Colgate University had a chance to examine the artifacts they returned the items to the Oneida Nation. The archaeologists spoke to reservation residents, showing slides of some of the three thousand items the students had found. Many of the artifacts were then put on display at the tribe's cultural center.

Canoe Museum

While some tribes are sponsoring archaeological digs to find out what is under the ground, other tribes are working to preserve items they already have. On the Nez Perce Reservation the tribal museum has undertaken a preservation project to repair four ancient canoes. These watercraft date back to a much more ancient time than the first contact between whites and the Nez Perce. "When we think of the Nez Perce traveling, we think of the horse culture," says museum curator Bob Chenoweth. "Well, that's what people have done for probably the last 200 years. But the other nine or 10,000 years people were traveling around in canoes."[80]

Because the tribe traveled on rivers that had rapids, they used sturdy canoes made from hollowed-out logs, not the bark-covered canoes used by tribes in the east. They usually did not chop down trees to make the canoes but instead recovered trees or logs that had fallen into the river.

The efforts to preserve the canoes include injecting a resin adhesive into the wood to hold the wood fibers together. The goal of the project is not to restore the canoes but rather to keep them from deteriorating from rot and fungus.

Bringing Them Home

Some preservation efforts are focused on repatriating human remains and sacred objects affiliated with a particular tribe. Human remains and funerary objects were often taken from tribal lands that were ceded to the federal government years ago. Many of these items ended up being stored in museum collections. A law passed in 1970, however, requires that ancestral remains housed in federally funded institutions be returned to tribes.

In 2002 Governor Malcolm Bowekaty, of the Zuni Pueblo in New Mexico, testifies at a Senate hearing on the protection of sites sacred to his tribe.

In Oregon tribal leaders from the Confederated Tribes of the Umatilla have been working with government agencies and the Smithsonian Institution to identify and recover ancestral remains and objects. In June 2003 the tribe held a ceremony to rebury the remains of 111 people in a common grave on the Umatilla Reservation. Those attending the ceremony included reservation leaders and tribal members as well as officials from a neighboring reservation and the Bureau of Indian Affairs. "The significance of the reburial is knowing that our ancestors are going to be at rest," says a Confederate Tribes of the Umatilla official, "but the effort we gave these ancestors for reburial also reflects the work tribes throughout the nation are doing and it reflects on the work we still need to do."[81]

Restoring Land

Many tribes are involved in efforts to ensure that sites that Native Americans have used for thousands of years are protected from mining operations, roads, electrical lines, and other development projects. Many tribes have filed lawsuits to keep non-Indians from building on

A thundering herd of mustangs races across a plain in South Dakota. Many tribes are reintroducing herds of wild animals on the reservations.

land that has been used for healing and ceremonies as well as burial mounds.

In traditional Native American culture, land, air, and water are considered gifts from the Creator. Therefore, Native Americans take seriously what they see as an obligation to care for the environment. As part of their stewardship, tribes work to prevent pollution and to restore areas that have become contaminated. On the Pine Ridge Reservation in South Dakota, for example, efforts are underway to dispose of ordnance located on reservation land that was used as an aerial bombing and gunnery range in World War II. The Badland Bombing Range Project (BBRP) has responsibility for clearing three hundred thousand acres that served as a practice range for both the U.S. Air Force and Army. "Our primary purpose is to reduce the existing and future threats to public health, welfare and the environment posed by the release of toxic substances and remaining unexploded ordnance,"[82] explains project director Emma Featherman Sam. The BBRP employs more than twenty members of the tribe. It is estimated it will take fifteen years to clean up the areas people are most likely to use in the future. The tribe plans to open a Lakota Heritage Education Center next to the bombing range.

Preservation efforts also focus on ensuring that development that does occur is culturally appropriate. On the Fort Apache Reservation, members of the White Mountain Apache tribe are replacing barbed wire fencing, which was introduced by white settlers in the middle of the nineteenth century, with a more traditional material. On the reservation the tribe is replacing the barbed wire with juniper posts. The posts will be cut by tribal members and finished at a tribal manufacturing plant.

Many tribes are also restoring wild animal herds to the reservation. On the River Sioux Reservation wild horses are once again running free. Horses are traditionally considered sacred to the Lakota people. The tribe has set aside twenty-one thousand acres on the reservation for a wildlife park, which includes a herd of two thousand buffalo and 120 mustangs, taken from Nevada's Virginia Range herd. The tribe accepted the horses as part of efforts to ensure that the herd does not become extinct. The wildlife preserve also includes elk, deer, and black-footed ferrets.

Traditional Games

Efforts at cultural preservation extend to bringing back traditional tribal sports. The result of these efforts is the International Traditional Games, which are held on various reservations each year. The games emphasize cooperation and teamwork rather than competition. The idea for the International Traditional Games competition came from a project by a group of students at Browning Middle School on the Blackfeet Reservation in 1989. To find out about traditional Blackfeet games, the students interviewed tribal elders and read historical documents and books.

The students learned about traditional games such as shinny and hoop and arrow, games that were the forerunners to sports such as hockey, lacrosse, and basketball. These traditional games, the students found, were an important part of tribal life. Arleen Adams, a member of the native games committee at Blackfeet College on the Blackfeet Reservation, explains how the games helped the tribal community: "Indian games taught unity that a people of a tribe could not survive without. Today, tribal unity is most heard of as teamwork."[83]

In 1999 the Blackfeet Reservation hosted the first International Traditional Games. The

Maintaining a cultural identity is important for all Native Americans. During a festival in British Columbia, Canada, men in war canoes participate in a traditional sport.

competition is like the Olympics in that it welcomes contestants from around the world, including the United States, Mexico, Canada, and New Zealand. But unlike the Olympics, the International Traditional Games encourage anyone who wishes to do so to participate in the contests. The competition even has "learning lodges" where people can go to learn how to play the various games.

Some of the games offer a twist to a familiar idea. For instance, in the "slowest horse" race, players bring their slowest horse and then swap horses with another player. The players then try to beat their own horse to the finish line.

Looking Ahead

Although the Blackfeet children were able to revive their long-lost traditional games, many Native American traditions and customs are in danger of being lost forever. Many Native Americans believe that there is still enough time to save their cultural identity but concede that the task will not be easy. In some cases tribes do not have enough money to undertake preservation efforts or there are few people who remember the old ways. Tribal leaders acknowledge that they must act quickly to preserve the knowledge of their elders and pass it down to the younger generation.

Despite the poverty and hardships associated with reservation life, many Native Americans feel a deep sense of pride in their cultural identity. "We're not rich in money and material stuff," says Rita Little Boy, who lives with her family in a small home on the Pine Ridge Reservation in South Dakota. "But we're rich in our life, in our language, our culture. We're rich in that."[84]

Notes

Introduction:
A Beautiful but Dangerous Isolation

1. Wyatt Buchanan, "Shoshone-Paiutes Enjoy Remoteness of Rez," *Sho-Ban News*, August 29, 2002, p. S16.
2. Quoted in Buchanan, "Shoshone-Paiutes Enjoy Remoteness of Rez."
3. Julie Schindler, interview with author, June 26, 2003.
4. Quoted in Tim Archulleta, "The State of Our Children: Age 10," *Albuquerque Tribune*, February 7, 2002. www.abqtrib.com/archives/news02/020702_news_age10.shtml.
5. Betty Reid and Maureen West, "Old and Alone on the Reservation," *Arizona Republic*, September 5, 1999. www.azcentral.com/news/reid/index.shtml.
6. Delphine Red Shirt, "Feeling at Home over 1,000 Miles Away," *Indian Country Today*, Nov. 6, 2002, p. D2.

Chapter 1:
A Host of Sovereign Governments

7. Anthony R. Pico, "Sovereignty Is Absolute for Native Nations," *Indian Country Today*, July 7, 1998, p. A5.
8. Minnesota Indian Affairs Council, *"Tribal Government: Teacher Background Information,"* April 2004. www.indians.state.mn.us/resources/govbkgnd.html.
9. Quoted in Ellen Chang, "Talk to Focus on Success of Indian Reservations," *Rice News*, March 29, 2001. www.rice.edu/projects/reno/rn/20010329/Templates/indian.html.
10. Sonia Weiss, "The Numbers Don't Lie; Money and Power Lead to Greed and Corruption on Pine Ridge," *Native Voice*, January 11, 2004, p. 1.
11. Quoted in Peggy Berryhill, "Hopi Potskwaniat: The Hopi Pathway to the Future," *Native Americas*, March 31, 1998, p. 31.
12. Quoted in S.J. Tanya Wilson Lee, "Maybe Someday—but Not Today; Tradition and Prophecy vs. Modern Conveniences in Old Oraibi," *News from Indian Country*, December 15, 2003, p. 10A.
13. Quoted in Lee, "Maybe Someday."
14. Quoted in James Hagengruber, "Traditional Cheyenne Leaders Fix Modern Problem," *Billings Gazette*, March 8, 2003. www.turtletrack.org/Issues03/Co03082003/co03082003_CheyenneLeaders.htm.
15. Quoted in Hagengruber, "Traditional Cheyenne Leaders Fix Modern Problem."
16. Quoted in Brenda Norrell, "Navajo Whistleblower Threatened," *Indian Country Today*, January 10, 2001, p. A2.
17. Quoted in Jim Camden, "Justices Visit Tribal Court," *Spokesman-Review*, July 19, 2001. www.turtletrack.org/Issues01/Co07282001/CO_07282001_Justices.htm.

Chapter 2: Education

18. Diane Weaver Dunne, "Teachers on Mission to Save Heritage," *Education World*, September 6, 2001. www.educationworld.com/a-issues/issues188.shtml.
19. Quoted in Joyce Riha Linik, "Seeking Native Teachers," *Northwest Education*,

Spring 2004. www.nwrel.org/ nwedu/09 03/seeking.php.

20. Quoted in Sararesa Begay, "'. . . They Rarely Ask Questions,'" *Navajo Times*, September 19, 2002, p. A1.

21. Jonathan Eig, "Keeping Hope: A Principal Battles Legacy of Failure at Indian School," *Wall Street Journal*, December 26, 2002, p. A1.

22. Quoted in Eig, "Keeping Hope."

23. Quoted in Ellen R. Delisio, "Native American Schools Ponder, Assail Dropout Rates," *Education World*, September 6, 2001. www.education-world. com/a_issues/issues190.shtml.

24. Quoted in Steve Lackmeyer, "16-Year-Old Adjusts to Life at Bacone," *Oklahoman*, December 2, 2000. www.turtle track.org/Issues00/Co12022000/CO_12 022000_Bacone.htm.

25. Quoted in Lackmeyer, "16-Year-Old Adjusts to Life at Bacone."

26. Quoted in Lackmeyer, "16-Year-Old Adjusts to Life at Bacone."

27. Quoted in *Indian Country Today*, "Nontraditional Colleges for Very Traditional People," May 4, 1998, p. B5.

28. Quoted in *Indian Country Today*, "Nontraditional Colleges for Very Traditional People."

29. Quoted in James G. Hill, "Bay Mills Community College Helps Native Americans Prepare for Life in Mainstream United States," *Detroit Free Press*, August 15, 2000.

30. Tom Nugent, "Tribal Colleges Drum Up Students," *Washington Post*, April 19, 2003, p. A03.

31. Nugent, "Tribal Colleges Drum Up Students."

Chapter 3: Making a Living

32. Quoted in Robert Struckman, "Indians Play Pivotal Role in Fighting Nation's Wildfires," *Christian Science Monitor*, May 16, 2001. http://search.csmonitor. com/durable/2001/05/16/fp2s2-csm.shtml.

33. Quoted in Marley Shebala, "Navajo Scouts Earn Recognition as One of Nation's Best," *Navajo Times*, February 17, 2000, p. A1.

34. Quoted in Robert Struckman, "Indians Play Pivotal Role in Fighting Nation's Wildfires," *Christian Science Monitor*, May 16, 2001.

35. Dorreen Yellow Bird, "A Healer Gladly Returns to Her People," *Canku Ota*, December 1, 2001. www.turtletrack. org/Issues01/Co12012001/CO_1201200 1_Healer.htm.

36. Quoted in Marley Shebala, "Hard Working Single Mothers Earn Their Transportation," *Navajo Times*, February 25, 1999, p. A1.

37. Quoted in Ruth Leper, "Ancestral Art," Sign On San Diego.com, October 19, 2002. www.turtletrack.org/Issues02/Co 10192002/CO_10192002_Ancestral_Art. htm.

38. Chet Barfield, "Ancestral Artistry," *San Diego Union-Tribune*, October 5, 2002. www.turtletrack.org/Issues02/Co100520 02/CO_10052002_Artistry.htm.

39. Quoted in *Navajo Times*, "Farmer Boasts of Traditional Ways," May 28, 1998, p. A7.

40. Quoted in Sararesa Begay, "Speakers Hail Return of Churro Sheep," *Navajo Times*, July 3, 2003, p. A6.

41. Quoted in Betty Reid, "Children Try to Walk Line Between Old, New, Bear Burden of Guilt," *Arizona Republic*, September 5, 1999. www.azcentral.com/ news/reid/index.shtml.

42. Quoted in Terry Wooster, "Tribes Return Bison to Circle of Life," *Canku*

Ota, July 29, 2000. www.turtletrack.org/Issues00/Co07292000/CO_07292000_Bison.htm.

43. Quoted in David Rooks, "Rides into the Heart," *Indian Country Today*, May 31, 2000, p. C3.

Chapter 4: Daily Life

44. Celesta Limberhand, "Dance of the People," *Spokesman Review*, August 12, 2000. www.turtletrack.org/Issues00/Co08122000/CO_08122000_Dance.htm.
45. Quoted in Gwen Florio, "Indians Longing for Shelter," *Denver Post*, January 22, 2003, p. A01.
46. Quoted in Nathan J. Tohtsoni, "Expansion: Boys and Girls Club to Grow from Two to 11," *Navajo Times*, April 19, 2001, p. A1.
47. Quoted in Jim Kent, "Big Bat's—At 'The Crossroads' to Lakota Culture," *News From Indian Country*, February 15, 2002, p. 16B.
48. Quoted in Kent, "Big Bat's."
49. Quoted in Julie Johnson, "Hoopa Valley Radio," *New California Media*, May 3, 2003. www.turtletrack.org/Issues03/Co05032003/CO_05032003_Radio.htm.
50. Quoted in Jim Kent, "Radio Vital Support in Indian Country," *Indian Country Today*, March 1, 1999, p. C3.
51. Catherine C. Robbins, "Indian Country Sends a Stronger Signal," *New York Times*, February 4, 2001, p. 2.33.
52. KILI Radio. www.lakotamall.com/kili.
53. Quoted in Diana Claitor, "Apache Radio Reports to People in Spite of Wildfire, Politics," *Indian Country Today*, October 2, 2002, p. D1.
54. Quoted in Frank Turco, "The Trials of Reservation Transit," *Bus Ride*, June 2003. www.busride.com/2003/06/The_trials_of_reservation_transit.asp.
55. Quoted in Turco, "The Trials of Reservation Transit."

Chapter 5: Beliefs, Ceremonies, and Celebrations

56. Quoted in Alecia Foster, "Lessons of a Cheyenne Tribe," *Los Angeles Times*, May 19, 2001. www.turtletrack.org/Issues01/Co05192001/CO_05192001_Lessons.htm.
57. Reid, "Children Try to Walk Line Between Old, New, Bear Burden of Guilt."
58. Quoted in Jenn Rudd, "Reversing a Cycle, Carrying a Tradition," *Native News*, 2004. www.umt.edu/journalism/about_us/student_work/nativenews02.com/stories/FortBelknap.html.
59. Suzanne Ruta, "Dances with Buffaloes," *Canku Ota*, December 30, 2000. www.turtletrack.org/Issues00/Co12302000/CO_12302000-Dance_Buffalo.htm.
60. Jay Fikes, "A Brief History of the Native American Church," in Huston Smith, *One Nation Under God*. San Francisco: Council on Spiritual Practices, 2004. www.csp.org/communities/docs/fikes-nac_history.html.
61. Ellen Gedalius, "The Ways of Tribal Court," Medill News Service, April 7, 2001. www.turtletrack.org/Issues01/Co04072001/CO_04072001_Courts.htm.
62. Quoted in Gedalius, "The Ways of Tribal Court."
63. Julia Roller, "Sweat Lodges in Wyoming," University of California Berkeley Graduate School of Journalism, Student Projects, 2004. http://journalism.berkeley.edu/projects/nm/julia/sweat.html.
64. Eig, "Keeping Hope."
65. Quoted in *Homeland: One Reservation, Three Years, Four Families*, video. Berkeley: University of California, Extension

Center for Media and Independent Learning, 1998.

66. Quoted in Jim Kent, "Graduating Students Step Back into Lakota Culture," *News from Indian Country*, June 15, 2001, p. 18A.

67. *Wind River News*, "Powwow: A Rich Heritage," July 9, 1998, p. S8.

68. *Wind River News*, "Tips for Enjoying a Powwow and Proper Etiquette," July 10, 1997, p. S1.

69. *Wind River News*, "Tips for Enjoying a Powwow and Proper Etiquette."

70. Ethel Winnipeg, "Powwow Trail: Telling Who's Who in the Powwow Circle," *Alberta Sweetgrass*, June 30, 1996, p. 9.

71. Limberhand, "Dance of the People."

72. Quoted in Maisie MacKinnon, "Canoe Journey Challenges the Heart and Soul," *Indian Country Today*, August 21, 2002, p. B1.

Chapter 6: Cultural Preservation

73. Quoted in Carrie Antlfinger, "New Life for Near-Dead Languages," *Houston Chronicle*, April 6, 2003, p. 6.

74. Quoted in Don Cox, "Native Americans Rediscover Lost Languages," *Reno Gazette-Journal*, February 10, 2001. www.turtletrack.org/Issues01/Co0210200 1/CO_02102001_Lostlanguage.htm.

75. Quoted in Karen Ivanova, "Institute Bringing Blackfeet Language into Next Century," *Great Falls Tribune*, April 20, 2002. www.turtletrack.org/

Issues02/Co04202002/CO_04202002_ Blackfeet_Institute.htm.

76. Quoted in Ivanova, "Institute Bringing Blackfeet Language into Next Century."

77. Quoted in *Canku Ota*, "Lemhi Shoshoni Creates Shoshoni Dictionary," April 21, 2001. www.turtletrack.org/Issues01/Co 04212001/CO_04212001_Shoshoni.htm.

78. Quoted in Carrie Moran McCleary, "Project Preserves Traditional Crow Site Names," *Indian Country Today*, January 13, 2001. www.turtletrack.org/ Issues01/Co01132001/CO_01132001_ Crow_Names.htm.

79. Quoted in Michelle Breidenbach, "Oneida Nation's History Uncovered," Syracuse Online, April 21, 2001. www.turtletrack.org/Issues01/Co072820 01/CO_07282001_Justices.htm.

80. Quoted in Rebecca Boone, "Nez Perce Museum Boasts Huge Collection of Ancient Canoes," *Lewiston Morning Tribune*, July 1, 2001. www.turtletrack. org/Issues01/Co07142001/CO_0714200 1_Canoes.htm.

81. Quoted in *Confederated Umatilla Journal*, "Remains Reburied, Reunited," July 31, 2003, p. 1.

82. Jim Kent, "Badlands Bombing Range Project Works to Restore Land," *News From Indian Country*, December 31, 2001, p. 12A.

83. Quoted in Leigh T. Jimmie, "Games Indians Play," *Native Voice*, January 24, 2003, p. 3.

84. Quoted in *Homeland*.

For Further Reading

Books

George Ancona, *Powwow*. San Diego, CA: Harcourt Brace Jovanovich, 1993. The book features a photo essay on the Crow Fair, one of the largest powwows in the United States. Beautiful color photographs and text tell about the dancers and event activities.

Walter Echo-Hawk and Roger C. Echo-Hawk, *Battlefields and Burial Grounds*. Minneapolis, MN: Lerner, 1996. Describes efforts by Native American tribes, especially the Pawnee, to recover and rebury the bones of their ancestors.

Kenji Kawano, *Warriors: Navajo Code Talkers*. Flagstaff, AZ: Northland, 1990. Beautifully illustrated book features photographs of the Navajo Code Talkers, a group of Navajos who developed and used a secret code that helped the U.S. military win key battles during World War Two.

Karen Liptak, *Native American Indian Tribal Chiefs*. New York: Franklin Watts, 1992. Profiles historic and contemporary chiefs including Chief Joseph, Sitting Bull, and Wilma Mankiller.

Christine Mather, *Native America: Arts, Traditions, and Celebrations*. New York: Clarkson Potter, 1990. Provides both color and black-and-white photographs of Native American arts, culture, and ceremonies. Also describes how young Native Americans are taught traditional crafts and ceremonies.

Web Sites

Encyclopedia of North American Indians (http://college.hmco.com). Provides a broad range of information on North American Indian tribes.

Native Culture (www.nativeculture.com). Offers links to resources in three categories: tribes and nations; arts and expression; and learning, teaching, and sharing information. Also includes articles on a variety of topics.

Storytellers: Native American Authors Online (www.hanksville.org/storytellers). Gives a listing of Native American authors and their works as well as their tribal affiliations. Provides links for additional information on storytelling.

Works Consulted

Periodicals

Carrie Antlfinger, "New Life for Near-Dead Languages," *Houston Chronicle*, April 6, 2003.

Sararesa Begay, "Speakers Hail Return of Churro Sheep," *Navajo Times*, July 3, 2003.

———, "'They Rarely Ask Questions,'" *Navajo Times*, September 19, 2002.

Peggy Berryhill, "Hopi Potskwaniat: The Hopi Pathway to the Future," *Native Americas*, March 31, 1998.

Paul Boyer, "Learning Lodge Institute," *Tribal College Journal of American Indian Higher Education*, May 31, 2000.

Wyatt Buchanan, "Shoshone-Paiutes Enjoy Remoteness of Rez," *Sho-Ban News*, August 29, 2002.

Confederated Umatilla Journal, "Remains Reburied, Reunited," July 31, 2003.

Diana Claitor, "Apache Radio Reports to People in Spite of Wildfire, Politics," *Indian Country Today*, October 2, 2002.

Jonathan Eig, "Keeping Hope: A Principal Battles Legacy of Failure at Indian School," *Wall Street Journal*, December 26, 2002.

Gwen Florio, "Indians Longing for Shelter," *Denver Post*, January 22, 2003.

Jennifer Hafner, "Traditional Shoshone Art of Basket Weaving Revived," *Wind River News*, September 16, 1999.

James G. Hill, "Bay Mills Community College Helps Native Americans Prepare for Life in Mainstream United States," *Detroit Free Press*, August 15, 2000.

Kay Humphrey, "A Child's Dream Becomes a Rare Exchange Between Two Cultures,"

Indian Country Today, August 8, 2001.

Indian Country Today, "Nontraditional Colleges for Very Traditional People," May 4, 1998.

Leigh T. Jimmie, "Games Indians Play," *Native Voice*, January 24, 2003. Jim Kent, "Badlands Bombing Range Project Works to Restore Land" *"News from Indian Country*, December 31, 2002.

———, "Big Bat's—At '"The Crossroads' to Lakota Culture," *News from Indian Country*, February 15, 2002.

———, "Crow Students Win National Science Competition," *Indian Country Today*, March 1, 1999.

———, "Graduating Students Step Back into Lakota Culture," *News from Indian Country*, June 15, 2001.

———, "Just Keep Dancing," *News from Indian Country*, November 30, 2002.

———, "Radio Vital Support in Indian Country," *Indian Country Today*, March 1, 1999.

S.J. Tanya Wilson Lee, "Maybe Someday—but Not Today; Tradition and Prophecy vs. Modern Conveniences in Old Oraibi," *News from Indian Country*, December 15, 2003.

Levi Long, "Indian Wells Elementary Sees Enrollment Boom," *Navajo Times*, August 8, 2003.

Maisie MacKinnon, "Canoe Journey Challenges the Heart and Soul," *Indian Country Today*, August 21, 2002.

Dan McDonald, "Remote Tribe Gets Mail the Old Fashioned Way," *Seminole Tribune*, October 1, 1999.

Rob McDonald, "Kalispels to Put on Opera," *Spokesman Review*, August 10, 2001.

Cate Montana, "Siletz Beader Uses Craft to Help Youth," *Indian Country Today*, December 27, 2000.

Navajo Times, "Farmer Boasts of Traditional Ways," May 28, 1998.

Brenda Norrell, "Navajo Whistleblower Threatened," *Indian Country Today*, January 10, 2001.

Tom Nugent, "Tribal Colleges Drum Up Students," *Washington Post*, April 19, 2003.

Anthony R. Pico, "Sovereignty Is Absolute for Native Nations," *Indian Country Today*, July 7, 1998.

Delphine Red Shirt, "Feeling at Home over 1,000 Miles Away," *Indian Country Today*, November 6, 2002.

Catherine C. Robbins, "Indian Country Sends a Stronger Signal," *New York Times*, February 4, 2001.

David Rooks, "Rides into the Heart," *Indian Country Today*, May 31, 2000.

Brenda Wade Schmidt, "Michigan BIA School Serves as Example," *Argus Leader*, January 26, 2004.

Ron Selden, "Blackfoot Veterinarian," *Indian Country Today*, March 29, 2000.

Marley Shebala, "Hard Working Single Mothers Earn Their Transportation," *Navajo Times*, February 25, 1999.

———, "Navajo Scouts Earn Recognition as One of Nation's Best," *Navajo Times*, February 17, 2000.

Valerie Taliman, "Termination by Bureaucracy," *Native Americas*, June 30, 2002.

Nathan J. Tohtsoni, "Expansion: Boys and Girls Club to Grow from Two to 11," *Navajo Times*, April 19, 2001.

Sonia Weiss, "The Numbers Don't Lie; Money and Power Lead to Greed and Corruption on Pine Ridge," *Native Voice*, January 11, 2004.

Wind River News, "Powwow: A Rich Heritage," July 9, 1998.

Wind River News, "Tips for Enjoying a Powwow and Proper Etiquette," July 10, 1997.

Ethel Winnipeg, "Powwow Trail: Telling Who's Who in the Powwow Circle," *Alberta Sweetgrass*, June 30, 1996.

Internet Sources

American Indian College Fund, "Who Is the College Fund?" 2003. www.aicf.org.

Tim Archulleta, "The State of Our Children: Age 10," *Albuquerque Tribune*, February 7, 2002. www.abqtrib.com/archives/news 02/020702_news_age10.shtml.

Chet Barfield, "Ancestral Artistry," *San Diego Union-Tribune*, October 5, 2002. www. turtletrack.org/Issues02/Co10052002/CO _10052002_Artistry.htm.

Rebecca Boone, "Nez Perce Museum Boasts Huge Collection of Ancient Canoes," *Lewiston Morning Tribune*, July 1, 2001. www.turtletrack.org/Issues01/Co0714200 1/CO_07142001_Canoes.htm.

Boys and Girls Clubs in Indian Country, "Facts," 2004. www.naclubs.org.

Michelle Breidenbach, "Oneida Nation's History Uncovered," Syracuse Online, April 21, 2001. www.turtletrack.org/Issues01/ Co04212001/CO_04212001_Oneida.htm.

Jim Camden, "Justices Visit Tribal Court," *Spokesman-Review*, July 19, 2001. www. turtletrack.org/Issues01/Co07282001/CO _07282001-Justices.htm.

Canku Ota, "Lemhi Shoshoni Creates Shoshoni Dictionary," April 21, 2001. www.turtletrack.org/Issues01/Co0421200 1/CO_04212001_Shoshoni.htm.

Ellen Chang, "Talk to Focus on Success of Indian Reservations," Rice News Service, March 29, 2001. www.rice.edu/projects/ reno/rn/20010329/Templates/indian.html.

Council of Indian Nations, "Southwest Indians Today: Education," 2004. www.cin programs.org.

Don Cox, "Native Americans Rediscover Lost Languages," *Reno Gazette-Journal*, February 10, 2001. www.turtletrack.org/Issues01/Co02102001/CO-02102001-Lost language.htm.

E.S. Curtis, "Nez Perce Museum Boasts Huge Collection of Ancient Canoes," *Lewiston Morning Tribune*, July 1, 2001. www.turtletrack.org/Issues01/Co0714200 1/CO_07142001_Canoes.htm.

Ellen R. Delisio, "Native American Schools Ponder, Assail Dropout Rates," *Education World*, September 6, 2001. www.education-world.com/a_issues/isues190.shtml.

Diane Weaver Dunne, "Teachers on Mission to Save Heritage," *Education World*, September 6, 2001. www.educationworld.com/a_issues/issues188.shtml.

Jay Fikes, "A Brief History of the Native American Church." In Huston Smith, *One Nation Under God.* San Francisco: Council on Spiritual Practices, 2004. www.csp.org/communities/docs/fikes-nac_history.html.

Alecia Foster, "Lessons of a Cheyenne Tribe," *Los Angeles Times*, May 19, 2001. www.turtletrack.org/Issues01/Co05192001/CO_05192001_Lessons.htm.

Ellen Gedalius, "The Ways of Tribal Court," Medill News Service, April 7, 2001. www.turtletrack.org/Issues01/Co0407200 1/CO_04072001_Courts.htm.

James Hagengruber, "Traditional Cheyenne Leaders Fix Modern Problem," *Billings Gazette*, March 8, 2003. www.turtletrack.org/Issues03/Co03082003/CO_030 82003_CheyenneLeaders.htm.

Scott Howard-Cooper, "Keeping in Touch," *Sacramento Bee*, January 13, 2001. www.turtletrack.org/Issues01/Co0113200 1/CO_01132001_Radio.htm.

InfoDome, "California Tribes and Their Reservations," 2004. http://infodome.sdsu.edu.

Karen Ivanova, "Institute Bringing Blackfeet Language into Next Century," *Great Falls Tribune*, April 20, 2002. www.turtletrack.org/Issues02/Co04202002/CO_042 02002_Blackfeet_Institute.htm.

Julie Johnson, "Hoopa Valley Radio," *New California Media*, May 3, 2003. www.turtletrack.org/Issues03/Co05032003/CO_05032003_Radio.htm.

Steve Lackmeyer, "16-Year-Old Adjusts to Life at Bacone," *Oklahoman*, December 2, 2000. www.turtletrack.org/Issues00/Co12022000/CO_12022000_Bacone.htm.

Ruth Leper, "Ancestral Art," Sign On San Diego.com October 19, 2002. www.turtletrack.org/Issues02/Co10192002/CO_101 92002_Ancestral_Art.htm.

Celesta Limberhand, "Dance of the People," *Spokesman Review*, August 12, 2000. www.turtletrack.org/Issues00/Co0812200 0/CO_08122000_Dance.htm.

Joyce Riha Linik, "Seeking Native Teachers," *Northwest Education*, Spring 2004. www.nwrel.org/nwedu/09-03/seeking.php.

Carrie Moran McCleary, "Project Preserves Traditional Crow Site Names," *Indian Country Today*, January 13, 2001. www.turtletrack.org/Issues01/Co01132001/CO_01132001_Crow_Names.htm.

Minnesota Indian Affairs Council, "*Tribal Government: Teacher Background Information,*" April 2004. www.indians.state.mn.us/resources/govbkgnd.html.

Office of Indian Education Program, "Our Schools," 2003. www.oiep.bia.edu.

Betty Reid, "Children Try to Walk Line Between Old, New, Bear Burden of Guilt," *Arizona Republic*, September 5, 1999. www.azcentral.com/news/reid/index.shtml.

Jenn Rudd, "Reversing a Cycle, Carrying a Tradition," *Native News*, 2004. www.umt.edu/journalism/about_us/student_work/nativenews02.com/stories/FortBelknap.html.

Suzanne Ruta, "Dances with Buffaloes," *Canku Ota*, December 30, 2000. www.turtletrack.org/Issues00/Co12302000/CO_12302000_Dance_Buffalo.htm.

Ron Shelden, "Slice of Buffalo Lung Beats Potato Chips Any Day," *Indian Country Today*, April 8, 2000. www.turtletrack.org/Issues00/Co04082000/CO_04082000_Buffalolung.htm.

Robert Struckman, "Indians Play Pivotal Role in Fighting Nation's Wildfires," *Christian Science Monitor*, May 16, 2001. http://search.csmonitor.com/durable/2001/05/16/fp2s2-csm.shtml.

Frank Turco, "The Trials of Reservation Transit," *Bus Ride*, June 2003. www.busride.com/2003/06/The_trials_of_reservation_transit.asp.

University of California Berkeley Graduate School of Journalism, Student Projects, "Sweat Lodges in Wyoming," 2004. http://journalism.berkeley.edu/projects/nm/julia/sweat.html.

Terry Wooster, "Tribes Return Bison to Circle of Life," *Canku Ota*, July 29, 2000. www.turtletrack.org/Issues00/Co07292000/CO_07292000_Bison.htm.

Dorreen Yellow Bird, "A Healer Gladly Returns to Her People," *Canku Ota*, December 1, 2001. www.turtletrack.org/Issues01/Col2012001/CO_12012001_Healer.htm.

Web Sites

KILI Radio (www.lakotamall.com/kili). The voice of the Lakota Nation, KILI radio is the largest Indian-owned-and-operated public radio station in America.

RezDog, 2004 (www.rezdog.com). Web site of the RezDog Clothing Company.

RezNet, 2004 (www.reznetnews.org). A news site featuring articles by Native American college students.

Video

Homeland: One Reservation, Three Years, Four Families. Berkeley: University of California, Extension Center for Media and Independent Learning, 1998.

Interview

Julie Schindler, interview with author, June 26, 2003. Former grade school teacher on Fort Belknap Reservation, Montana.

Index

Picture Credits

Cover photo: © Pete Saloutos/CORBIS
© John Annerino/Landov, 85
AP/Wide World Photos, 12, 14, 24, 25, 56, 62, 78, 84, 87, 89
© Art Today, Inc., 49, 77
© Craig Aurness/CORBIS, 53
Eddie Brady/Lonely Planet Images, 82
Comstock, Inc., 47
© Jim Erickson/CORBIS, 55
© Kevin Fleming/CORBIS, 21, 45
© Natalie Fobes/CORBIS, 88
© Foxwoods via Bloomberg News/Landov, 50
© Jeff Greenberg/Photo Edit, 59
© Ed Kashi/CORBIS, 26, 29

© Danny Lehman/CORBIS, 68–69
© Gunter Marx/Photography/CORBIS, 92
© Reuters/Landov, 40
© Bob Rowan; Progressive Image/CORBIS, 18, 41
© Pablo San Juan/CORBIS, 64
© Phil Schermeister/CORBIS, 37, 43, 81
© Michael T. Sedam/CORBIS, 51
© Paul A. Souders/CORBIS, 11
© Swift/Nanuga Images/CORBIS, 74
© Thomas Wiewandt; Visions of America/CORBIS, 90
© Marilyn "Angel" Wynn/Nativestock.com, 19, 30, 34, 36, 39, 67, 70, 71

About the Author

Katherine Wagner lives in Chicago, Illinois, where she enjoys visiting the city's many ethnic neighborhoods and learning about different cultures. She has bicycled through China and been a volunteer on an archaeological dig in French Polynesia. Before she started writing books for children, she worked as a general assignment reporter at a weekly newspaper in Georgia. She is the author of *Life in an Amish Community*, another book in Lucent's The Way People Live series.